Shellfish

Shellfish

50 Seafood Recipes for Shrimp, Crab, Mussels,
Clams, Oysters, Scallops, and Lobster

Cynthia Nims

Photography by Jim Henkens

SASQUATCH BOOKS

SEATTLE

To all the seafood fanatics in my life: those I've had the good fortune to learn from, be inspired by, travel with, and—above all—sit alongside for countless fabulous meals over the years. Here's to much more of the same.

Contents

Introduction

At a cookbook signing years ago, a gentleman walked up to my table, glanced at the cover of my book, and said, more or less, "Why would anyone need a crab cookbook? All you have to do is steam it and eat it!" I don't recall how I responded in that moment, but I've thought often about that remark and how—at a basic level—he was absolutely right. When shellfish is at its best, the less you do, the better. Steam, grill, or pan-fry with minimal accoutrements, and you've got an unparalleled feast.

So why did I sit down to write this book, knowing that to be true? For the simple fact that we're not all lucky enough to have the comfort level with shellfish to simply wing it when the opportunity presents itself. In light of that, this book covers some basics of sourcing and handling seven types of shellfish, and a selection of recipes to showcase each with a range of techniques and ingredients. Plus, I'm certain that even those who have an abundance of fresh-from-the-water shellfish to cook like to change things up now and again. You know what they say about variety.

I'm a lifelong Northwesterner who was fortunate to land a great magazine editing gig right out of culinary school. By the time my stint at *Simply Seafood* magazine was done, I had traveled to Kodiak Island in Alaska; Veracruz, Mexico; and Hawaii—among other fabulous destinations—for stories about outstanding seafood. I also interacted with an array of inspiring seafood experts, including many amazing chefs. I ate it *all* up, literally and figuratively.

In the years since that job, I've had countless shellfish adventures large and small, close to home and far afield—from slurping oysters on a Puget Sound beach late-night in midwinter to procuring littleneck clams at the source while on Virginia's Eastern Shore, to enjoying enormous shrimp and gooseneck barnacles at a sixty-plus-year-old restaurant in Lisbon. I've eaten so very many great meals, both dining out and home-cooked, featuring outstanding shellfish. It has all contributed to perspectives about, and an enduring enthusiasm for, cooking shellfish that I'll be sharing with you here. Of my many thoughts about shellfish, three themes rise to the top.

First, with each bite, we have a chance to appreciate just how distinctly delicious each type of shellfish is. Exploring the range of flavors and forms among the shellfish clan is a worthy pursuit. In our kitchens, this can mean branching out from the shellfish we're most familiar with to try new things. Venture to ask about selections you're not familiar with at the seafood counter and give them a try. If you've only tried a favorite shellfish fried in the past, give it a go grilled next time. When traveling, order a different type of shellfish you don't see at home, for both the pleasure of trying something new and adding another layer of local experience to the trip.

Second, the options for cooking (or not cooking, as the case may be) shellfish are seemingly endless. Shellfish can be dressed up or served casually, they work with most any cooking technique, they can be in-shell or not, they can be perfect for a weeknight supper or for a special occasion. With basic building blocks of cooking technique and familiarity with handling different types of shellfish, your shellfish repertoire will know no bounds.

Third, and I think most importantly, shellfish are naturally evocative creatures. From the way they look to how and where they grow to regions and cultures where they've been rooted for many generations, they are undeniably delicious little storytellers. We benefit from taking a moment to consider that story. It can be simply a matter of going from generic "clams" or "shrimp" to learning of different species and where they come from, maybe how they were caught or raised. I contend that a little backstory can make the dining experience more delectable, more memorable, richer.

While "family" has a specific taxonomic meaning in the scientific world, for the purposes of this book, I think of each chapter as a family of shellfish. The shellfish covered here fall into two groups: crustaceans (crab, shrimp, and lobster) and bivalves (clams, mussels, oysters, and scallops).

Within these chapters, I focus on shellfish species that I expect are likely to be available to most readers across the United States. Some others that you might come across—either occasionally in a specialty store or in narrower regional availability—will get a brief nod. I also offer shopping and storing tips, general cooking approaches, and a handful of recipes to exemplify some of that shellfish's delicious and varied possibilities.

Each of these families are worthy of their own spotlight, and there are books that showcase them individually. Including a couple of my own: one about oysters, another featuring crab. This collection covers more shellfish in smaller bites to fuel the general enjoyment of cooking shellfish at home and a broad appreciation for shellfish overall.

Shellfish Basics

It's been interesting to hear friends remark now and then that though they eat shellfish in restaurants pretty regularly, they seldom cook shellfish at home (echoing a national habit I've seen referenced a few times: many leave seafood cooking to the professionals). When they do prepare shellfish at home, it's often just one or two types, those they feel most confident cooking, likely from simple repetition if nothing else.

I can imagine the vicious cycle that traps some home cooks: cooking shellfish seems intimidating, so they don't buy it very often to cook at home, so they don't have a chance to get more comfortable with cooking shellfish, so they rarely buy shellfish to cook at home, and so on. If that sounds familiar, I hope to help break that cycle, with information and encouragement to make the prospect seem a bit less daunting. The recipes include a number of ideal entry-level preparations for first-time shellfish cooks.

Whether it's an initial introduction or a refresher, this chapter includes some tips for buying shellfish, an overview of ideal shellfish-cooking techniques, and discussion of some of my favorite ingredients to pair with shellfish. And when it comes to sourcing shellfish, take some comfort in knowing that living far from a coastline does not leave you out of the fun.

As noted earlier, preparing a great shellfish meal can be as easy as finding high-quality shellfish and cooking it simply, minimally adorned. At least as a starting point, beyond which there are endless possibilities for specific dishes to create. Your shellfish-cooking repertoire will grow quickly by applying different cooking techniques and incorporating flavors that can range from mellower citrus and herbal to bolder spicy and piquant.

Tips for Finding the Best

First off, I want to dispel the idea that access to great shellfish is limited to those of us who can smell the briny sea air from our front doors. Top-quality seafood shops—and well-stocked seafood counters within grocery stores—can be found across the country. Shellfish travel quite well, whether to a local store or even to your doorstep, with direct fisher- or farmer-to-consumer options. It might take a bit of work if you're not already familiar with shopping options near you. But it'll be worth the effort.

You will find shellfish sold in a range of forms, from live to frozen. Tips for selecting them vary with the species, and this is covered in more detail in the following chapters. Here are some general things to keep in mind.

A pretty seafood case doesn't necessarily mean better-quality shellfish, but it's one indication of care being taken with the product. Shellfish should be on or in ice or otherwise clearly well chilled. There may even be tanks holding live crab, oysters, or lobster. Ask questions if anything's unclear: what species it is, where it's from, if it's been previously frozen (not a bad thing at all, just something to know). If the person helping you doesn't have the answer and doesn't offer to find out for you, in my mind that leaves a big question mark. And I might move on to find something else for dinner.

I dislike the term "fishy" in the context of what poor quality seafood smells like, as if smelling of fish is inherently undesirable. Good fish, and shellfish, should smell of the ocean at high tide:

brisk, clean, a little briny; sometimes I find it has little aroma at all. Skip shellfish that has an aroma that is sour, funky, ammonia-like, or otherwise off.

"Fresh" is a squishy concept. Does it mean "never frozen"? Or "currently not in a frozen state"? Or "out of the water for less than a day"? It's hard to know without clarification from whoever's using the term. Ultimately, quality is the overriding goal. Frozen is preferable to a "fresh" piece of shellfish that's been lingering in the case a bit too long.

Done well, freezing preserves the quality of the shellfish shortly after harvest—sometimes done within a matter of hours. Commercial operations do this freezing at far lower temperatures than our home freezers can attain. Buying shellfish frozen makes many varieties available year-round and gives you some leeway before needing to cook it.

Any ice crystals on the surface should be very tiny, if visible at all; larger crystals (like you might see on ice cream that's hung around in the freezer too long) can indicate less-than-ideal handling. And avoid frozen shellfish with dry, opaque patches that can indicate freezer burn. If you see something in the case that's noted as previously frozen and you like the idea of having some to hold for cooking down the line, it's worth asking if they have some still frozen that you can buy.

Be sure to plan ahead and allow time for frozen shellfish to thaw slowly in the refrigerator overnight; it's the best way to preserve the quality of the shellfish. I like to do so in a colander set over a bowl so the shellfish aren't soaking in the water released as they thaw.

Your shellfish need to stay good and cold on the way home. If it's a warm day or the trip home's not a quick one, plan ahead and take along a cooler with frozen gel packs, or ask at the seafood counter if they can give you a bag of ice to tuck alongside the shellfish.

Be sure any shellfish you buy frozen stays frozen, getting it into the freezer as soon as possible. Don't try to refreeze thawed frozen shellfish: the quality will be significantly reduced.

Cooking Shellfish

I have designed the recipes here to be as versatile as possible, allowing you to use varieties of shellfish available to you. So I call for "medium clams" or "crabmeat" or "large shrimp" for the most part, rather than specific species, with just a few exceptions.

The beauty of shellfish, which you'll see expressed here often, is how easy it is to cook. I know there can be a lingering intimidation factor, not wanting to mess up that lovely, sometimes pricey, shellfish you brought home. But I believe you'll find shellfish to be a little more forgiving than you might have thought. And for the most part, shellfish cook quickly; so as long as it's not a more elaborate preparation, dinner can be on the table lickety-split.

TECHNIQUES

With a pot, some heat, and a bit of liquid, steaming is a go-to technique for shellfish. You can use water, wine, beer, or hard cider, with or without herbs, garlic, other aromatic elements. This is ideal for clams and mussels (tossed in the pot directly) as well as crab, lobster, and shrimp (perched on a basket or rack above the steaming liquids).

Boiling crab and lobster is another option, but I much prefer steaming. It takes far less time to bring a couple of inches of water to a boil than it does a full pot. And you don't have to worry about just the right amount of water: enough to be sure the shellfish will be submerged but not too much to risk overflow when they're added to the pot.

All these shellfish are outstanding grilling options too. Oysters in their shells, pre-shucked or not. Clams and mussels in a foil pouch or cast-iron pan, or directly on the grill if large enough. Crab and lobster grilled in their shells; scallops and shrimp threaded on skewers.

Baking and roasting are great all-season techniques that, like grilling, work well with shellfish in or out of their shells. And these methods can be just as easy: shellfish plus a bit of seasoning and a good dose of heat is all it takes.

There are many ways to fry, from a light stir-fry to more indulgent deep-frying. In between is frying in a shallow layer of oil, the quintessential expression of which, for me, is pan-fried oysters. Less oil and a hotter pan make way for searing, an ideal option for large sea scallops.

And cooking isn't even required for some shellfish. Just check out the offerings at your favorite oyster bar to know how beloved is the simplicity of an oyster slurped from its freshly shucked shell. East Coasters love their half-shell raw clams too. Scallops and shrimp appear in ceviche and similar preparations that are essentially raw, with lime juice or other acidic elements transforming—but not cooking—the flesh.

If you end up with leftover cooked shellfish after a meal, it should hold well for a day or two in the fridge. In the case of clams and mussels, take the meats from the shells. If you have the steaming liquid, strain it and store the meats in that liquid; otherwise just store as is, covered. Cooked crab, shrimp, and lobster meat should be stored in an airtight container; I prefer to take them out of the shell before storing so that they are ready to use the next day.

There are so many great options for those leftovers. In fact, many recipes here use cooked shellfish, so you'll find lots of inspiration for using leftover shellfish, whether on mini pizzas, in hearty salads, or in a dip for chips. Beyond those, think about embellishing some of your favorite recipes. Lobster quesadillas? Crab mac and cheese? Mussels tossed in curried vegetables? So many possibilities.

GETTING READY

The fancy-sounding French phrase *mise en place* (*meez ahn plahss*) is one of the best habits to develop when cooking. It simply means to put things in their place—more specifically, to account for and set up everything needed for a recipe before you dive in to begin cooking. I'd argue that it also includes carefully reading the whole recipe—not just a glance at ingredients for your shopping list and checking the cooking time to plan your schedule.

An important aspect of mise en place is addressing details mentioned in the ingredient list, such as cleaning and slicing leeks. When it comes time to add leeks to the skillet, they'll be ready to go, rather than needing to halt the cooking process so you can prep them at that moment. Or, oops, those eggs were supposed to be hard-cooked? Similarly, reading through the instructions ahead of time helps avoid surprises, such as a "set aside to cool" that throws off your timing. Taking the extra time for advanced preparation of the recipe makes the cooking process as smooth and uninterrupted as possible once you get under way.

EQUIPMENT

For the most part, cooking shellfish requires little in the way of specialty kitchen equipment. One exception would be an oyster knife for shucking oysters. I don't advise attempting that with any other knife. Good oyster knives are designed to be sturdy enough to withstand the pressure needed to pry apart the shells, with just enough of an edge to facilitate severing the adductor muscle from the shells, not sharp like our kitchen knives. There are lots of beautiful oyster knives to choose from these days. The workhorse in my collection is a style pro shuckers use, with a long, slender blade. This is the type you'll often find available from oyster farms when you're buying a dozen or two of their delicious product. They typically have a sturdy plastic handle with a bit of texture to help ensure a good grip even when your hand's a bit wet. Shucking isn't complicated but does require care: go slow and easy to get the hang of it (see page 90).

Another less-common item is an extra-large two-part steamer made for steaming seafood—particularly useful when a few or more live lobster or crab are on the menu. The bottom portion holds the liquids used for steaming, the deep top portion has a perforated base that allows steam to rise through the shellfish for cooking. I don't use the one I have all that often (and no recipe in this book relies on one), but it is handy when the occasion calls for it. Otherwise, I use a collapsible steamer basket in the bottom of my largest stock pot, usually big enough for a couple of whole crab or lobster at a time. If you don't have a pot quite that large, you can steam in batches, planning dinner time accordingly.

Long-handled tongs are helpful for maneuvering shellfish—particularly whole crab and lobster—in and out of their steaming pots, as well as handling shellfish on the grill. (Those may be two different sets of tongs.)

To get meat out of crab and lobster shells, there are crackers and mallets made for the purpose, plus slender picks and seafood forks to help extract the meat. A small pair of kitchen shears (some are made with shellfish in mind) can be helpful too, particularly with lobster and king and snow crab legs, cutting the length of the shell to easily expose the meat.

Otherwise, you probably have most of the equipment needed to accomplish a lot of great shellfish cooking already. A medium pot gets a lot of use, particularly for steaming clams and mussels; that pot could be a saucepan, Dutch oven, or similar vessel of 5- to 6-quart capacity or so. And a small, sturdy scrub brush to clean shells comes in handy too.

INGREDIENTS

Not only are shellfish versatile in terms of cooking techniques, they play well with plenty of other ingredients also. Here are some items that I turn to most often when cooking shellfish:

- Citrus, of course: it can be tempting to finish every dish with a spritz of lemon—the bright acidity is such a perfect complement to shellfish. Lemon, grapefruit, and other citrus get good play here.
- That acidic element comes in other forms too: vinegar is an easy choice; capers, tomatoes, and yogurt also bring contrasting acidity.
- Bright, aromatic flavors of fresh herbs, ginger, and garlic are well suited to shellfish; and while a number of onion types are used throughout the recipes, I find myself reaching for green onions and leeks often.
- Peppery and piquant flavors complement shellfish well, showing up with ingredients such as horseradish, chiles, peppery greens, wasabi.
- Butter (which I love dearly) is a particularly great partner for shellfish, whether for cooking—in a skillet or spooned on top before grilling—or as a finishing touch at the table in the form of a sauce or topping.

SAVE YOUR SHELLS!

A number of the recipes call for Shellfish Stock (page 183), whether as one of a few optional ingredients or—as in the case of Lobster and Artichoke Stew (page 150)—more of a key component. So your first assignment, should you accept it, is to cook some meals starting with in-shell shrimp, crab, and/or lobster. Rinse and save the shells, tucking them in an airtight container for the freezer if not using them right away, so you can accumulate what you need with other shells later. Or just make a smaller batch, using however many shells you have. You'll be very happy to later have portions of shellfish stock to pull from the freezer for future recipes.

Sustainability

There is a simple fact that no matter how seemingly mundane or ubiquitous a type of shellfish may be, every piece we purchase came from some stretch of water in some particular part of the globe. Contemplating where it came from and considering how it was caught or raised can help us make more thoughtful choices at the seafood counter. Even if only to become more aware that we *have* choices.

It is possible that, without even trying, you've been buying more shellfish that's considered sustainable than you were ten or fifteen years ago. There is so much more attention now on sustainability, with increasing consumer interest in knowing more about the food we eat, and rising demand for transparency as to where and how it was grown/harvested/produced. Seafood is a prime category for that interest.

A number of factors are considered regarding the sustainability of a particular seafood. These criteria include the specific species, how healthy its population is, the location of the harvest, how it was harvested or grown, and the impact on other species. These variables explain why few seafoods have a blanket thumbs-up or thumbs-down status with sustainability-focused organizations. It may be that a seafood caught in one region is an ideal choice, while the same species from another region is less so. And some seafoods may meet a number of sustainability criteria, but fall short on a couple others, getting a mixed review of sorts.

Broadly, buying from fisheries in the United States is considered a good starting point, given programs and regulations in place that set a foundation for sustainability standards. The majority of the seafood we consume in the United States, however, is imported, and the practices of related fisheries cover the gamut from sustainable—some certified as such—to troubling.

There seem to be more and more programs and organizations with a global scope helping to draw attention to, and improve, the overall sustainability of seafood harvesting around the world, not to mention ongoing research and technological advances. As a consumer (even as a writer!) it can be hard to keep track of the latest considerations in this very dynamic industry. You can dig in to do your own research if it's of interest, and ask questions of those supplying the seafood to you. Working with seafood on a daily basis, they may have insights to share.

Some seafood markets, and seafood departments within larger stores, make clear their focus on sustainable products, whether stating those commitments on in-store displays, on their website, or through other channels. And signage in the display case or information shared elsewhere may cite a specific reference to sustainability, perhaps MSC (Marine Stewardship Council) or BAP (Best Aquaculture Practices) certification, a Monterey Bay Aquarium Seafood Watch rating, or a designation from other organizations associated with monitoring sustainability practices.

It may not be feasible to choose the most sustainable shellfish on every trip to the market. I try but don't hit it 100 percent of the time. Making even a brief mental connection between the shellfish we cook and where it came from adds to an overall appreciation of the sources of the shellfish we eat. And it's a step that works toward assuring those shellfish populations thrive for generations to come.

Clams

This is one easy-going family of shellfish. Clams take little work to prep, and all you need is a pot, some heat, maybe a splash of wine or beer, and ten minutes or so to get dinner on the table. I imagine this ease is partly why clams have ranked among the top ten seafoods consumed in the United States for a number of years. That's a lot of steamed clams, pots of chowder, and countless other ways that clams are enjoyed.

The hard-shell clam varieties most commonly seen in stores are Manila clams from the West Coast and those known also as quahogs from the East Coast. Manila clams vary in size somewhat, but not nearly as much as do East Coast clams, which warrant a range of size grades. The smallest of them, littleneck, is on par with larger Manila clams. Going up from there, bigger grades include middleneck, cherrystone, and chowder. Having eaten mostly Manila clams for so many years, I was startled one day when my neighborhood grocery store in Seattle had huge East Coast clams in the case. A shopper next to me was giddy at the prospect of taking some home to cook. I couldn't get over the fact that just four clams weighed nearly one and a quarter pounds. I steamed, chopped, and stuffed them for a new-to-me treat.

There are a number of other clams you may see that have limited regional and seasonal availability. West Coast examples include the Pacific littleneck, a different species from the East Coast's, and the strikingly outsize geoduck (*gooey-duck*) clam, which can weigh as much as ten pounds (typically harvested at one to two pounds or so). Any clam that's steamed might be thought of as a "steamer," but in New England it references a specific species, also known as soft-shell clams. They have thinner (not really "soft") shells, primarily enjoyed simply steamed or breaded and fried. Different enough from hard-shell clams, they're not interchangeable in the recipes here.

Both coasts have a razor clam as well: the East Coast's version is more narrow and long, the West Coast's a bit shorter with an elongated oval shape. Mahogany and savory are among other clam types you might see on occasion.

While some clam harvesting today remains wild, most of what we see in stores has been farm-raised, which results in rather steady availability throughout the year.

Shopping and Storing

Manila clams are generally sold by the pound, either bulk or in mesh bags of a preset weight. Littleneck clams and other East Coast hard-shell clams may be sold by the pound or by the piece, either bulk or in set quantities by the bag.

Clams you buy fresh in the shell are alive and need to stay alive until you cook them. It's best to get them home and in the fridge as quickly as you can. If it's a warm day or it'll be a while before you get home, ask for a small bag of ice at the seafood counter to accompany your shellfish. Or plan ahead and have a cooler with frozen gel packs in the car.

Transfer the clams to a large bowl when you get home. I usually put them in a colander set inside the bowl to hold them above any liquid that accumulates. Top the clams with a damp, but not sopping wet, kitchen towel. The clams need air to survive, so don't cover the bowl any more than that.

Don't be tempted to store clams in water. Keeping them moist is one thing, but they will perish if submerged in fresh water for too long. If the towel dries out, dampen it again. It's ideal to cook clams the same day you buy them, but stored well, they should hold for a day or two.

Cleaning

Clams should be cleaned just before cooking. To do so, put them in a sturdy colander and shake them vigorously under cold running water for a minute or two. If you still feel grit or sand on the shells, pull out a brush to scrub them. You can always do a test: scrub a couple of shells and see if there's a visible difference in grit being removed.

As you're cleaning the clams, discard any with broken shells. Also make sure the shells are tightly closed: tap any gaping clams on the counter to see that they close completely. If not, discard them.

Cooking

Clams are the perfect casual meal that can be on the table in no time, with a salad alongside and obligatory bread to help soak up the flavorful liquids. From simple wine and garlic to citrus and herb accents to zesty chile-tomato mixtures, the steaming components have countless potential variations. Beyond that classic preparation, clams can be grilled, roasted, and sautéed in the shell, with many possibilities out of the shell. Among recipes here are steamed clams, clam-topped pizzas, clams stuffed for baking, and a rather classic chowder.

Manilas are on the smaller end of the scale, perfect for steaming to serve in the shell, and the cooked meats can be used whole in soups, pastas, and such. Larger East Coast hard-shell clams are also versatile, with smaller clams used for simpler steamed recipes, and the meats of larger clams often chopped to use in recipes such as chowders, fritters, and stuffed clams.

One thing about the different varieties of clams I noticed while testing is that the East Coast hard-shell clams had heavier shells than did the Manilas. So one pound of littlenecks usually produced a little less meat than a pound of Manila clams. The amount of clam meat you end up with in these recipes may vary depending on which clam you use.

Clam Chowder

with Petite Peas

As much as I love bacon and often include it in chowders, this version skips it to emphasize the briny-sweet flavor of the clams. This is a lighter style of chowder, just moderately thickened with a bit of flour. If you want to keep some of the clams in their shells for serving, feel free. How about enjoying another classic alongside: grilled cheese?

Makes 4 to 6 servings

- 2½ to 3 pounds small to medium live hard-shell clams, well rinsed (see page 17)
- 1½ cups water
- About 2 cups clam juice (see page 22), Shellfish Stock (page 183), or water
- ¼ cup unsalted butter
- 1 large leek, trimmed, cleaned (see page 48), and thinly sliced (about 1½ cups)
- 1 large carrot, cut into ¼-inch dice (about 1 cup)
- 2 stalks celery, thinly sliced (about ¾ cup)
- 2 tablespoons all-purpose flour
- 1½ teaspoons minced fresh thyme, or ½ teaspoon dried thyme
- 6 ounces red new potatoes, scrubbed and cut into ½-inch dice
- 1 cup thawed frozen petite peas
- 1 cup half-and-half
- Kosher salt and freshly ground black pepper

1   Put the clams and water in a medium pot, set the pot over medium-high heat, and cover. After 2 to 3 minutes, gently stir the clams with a large slotted spoon. Cover the pot and continue cooking, stirring once or twice more, until all, or mostly all, of the clams have opened, 2 to 5 minutes longer. Use the slotted spoon to transfer the opened clams to a large bowl. Continue cooking any remaining clams for 1 to 2 minutes, but discard any not opened after that time. If the liquids boil vigorously at any point, reduce the heat a bit. →

2   Pour the cooking liquids from the pot through a small fine-mesh sieve into a 4-cup measuring cup, leaving behind any grit in the bottom of the pot. When the clams are cool enough to handle, remove the meats. Add the liquids from the bottom of the bowl to those from the pot. Add enough clam juice to make 4 cups.

3   In the same pot (washed) or another soup pot, melt the butter over medium heat. Add the leek, carrot, and celery and cook, stirring occasionally, until tender (the carrot may not be fully tender), 5 to 7 minutes. Sprinkle the flour into the pot and cook for 2 minutes, stirring frequently to evenly distribute with the vegetables. Stir in the clam juice mixture and thyme, then add the potatoes. Simmer gently, stirring occasionally, until the potatoes are tender, 12 to 15 minutes; reduce the heat if needed to keep the liquid from boiling. The chowder will thicken a bit as it cooks.

4   While the chowder is simmering, chop the clams, though small clams can be used as is if you like.

5   Once the potatoes are tender, reduce the heat to medium-low and add the clams, peas, and half-and-half. Simmer gently until heated through, 3 to 5 minutes, taking care to avoid boiling or it may curdle a bit (still perfectly fine). Season to taste with salt and pepper, then ladle the chowder into individual bowls and serve right away.

CLAM JUICE

Also known as clam broth and clam nectar, this is essentially a by-product of cooking clams, capturing the briny essence they give off. If the recipe you're making doesn't need all—if any—of the cooking liquid left in the pot after steaming clams, it's a shame to toss it out. Strain the liquid through a small fine-mesh sieve, leaving any grit behind in the bottom of the pot. Let cool completely, then store in an airtight container and refrigerate for a couple of days, or freeze for a few months. The clam juice is ideal in Clam Chowder with Petite Peas (page 21), other seafood soups or stews, seafood risotto, and other places where its distinct briny sea flavor would be a welcome addition. Commercial clam juice is a good shortcut. Sometimes I'll mix clam juice with water to temper the strength of its flavor depending on the use.

Hard-Cider Steamed Clams

Beer is a common steaming partner for clams and mussels—always a solid choice. With a growing selection of great hard ciders available, it just gives us more options to play with. For cooking, I prefer to stick with simpler types of hard cider that are on the dry side.

Makes 2 to 4 servings

- 8 green onions, trimmed
- 2 tablespoons mild olive oil
- 2 cloves garlic, minced or pressed
- 1 bay leaf, preferably fresh, broken or torn in half
- 3 pounds small to medium live hard-shell clams, well rinsed (see page 17)
- 1 cup dry hard cider
- Sliced baguette or other bread, for serving

1   Slice the white and light-green parts of the green onions to cook with the clams. Thinly slice enough of the green tops to measure about ¼ cup and set aside to use as a garnish.

2   Heat the oil in a medium pot over medium heat. Add the white and light-green parts of the green onions, garlic, and bay leaf and cook, stirring occasionally, until the green onion is tender, 2 to 3 minutes. Add the clams and hard cider, increase the heat to medium-high, and cover. After 2 to 3 minutes, gently stir the clams with a large slotted spoon. Cover the pot and continue cooking, stirring once or twice more, until all, or mostly all, of the clams have opened, 2 to 5 minutes longer. If the liquids boil vigorously at any point, reduce the heat a bit.

3   Scoop the clams and cooking liquids into shallow bowls, discarding any clams that did not open (along with the bay leaf) and leaving any grit behind in the bottom of the pot. Scatter the sliced green onion tops over the clams and serve right away, with bread alongside.

Steamed Clams
with a Frenzy of Herbs

This "frenzy" describes a generous addition of tender herbs to the pot, an array more varied in the height of summer, when herbs flourish in our gardens. It's easy to go through a pound or more of clams per person when this dish is served as a meal with crusty bread and a favorite salad alongside. Depending on your appetite and how this is served (lunch, appetizer, lighter meal), the amount per person can vary.

Makes 2 to 4 servings

- 1¼ cups loosely packed tender fresh herbs, divided (see note)
- 3 tablespoons unsalted butter
- ⅓ cup thinly sliced shallot
- 1 tablespoon finely chopped rosemary (optional)

- 3 pounds small to medium live hard-shell clams, well rinsed (see page 17)
- ½ cup dry white wine or water
- Sliced baguette or other bread, for serving

1   Toss together the tender herbs in a small bowl.

2   Melt the butter in a medium pot over medium heat. Add the shallot and rosemary and cook, stirring occasionally, until the shallot is tender and lightly browned, 2 to 3 minutes. Add the clams and wine, cover, and increase the heat to medium-high. After 2 to 3 minutes, add 1 cup of the herbs and gently stir the clams with a large slotted spoon. Cover and continue cooking, stirring once or twice more, until all, or mostly all, of the clams have opened, 2 to 5 minutes longer. If the liquids boil vigorously at any point, reduce the heat a bit.

3   Scoop the clams, herbs, and cooking liquids into shallow bowls, discarding any clams that did not open and leaving any grit behind in the bottom of the pot. Top with the remaining herbs and serve right away, with bread alongside. →

NOTE: Herbs I've used include chives, thyme, shiso, tarragon, bronze fennel, parsley, cilantro, and basil. Select just three or four for this dish, but if you don't have a selection on hand, don't feel obligated to purchase multiple bundles. "Frenzy" could just as well be a whole lot of parsley—an herb I don't think gets nearly enough opportunity to shine on its own. (Have you tried parsley pesto? See page 173.) Small tender leaves can remain whole, larger leaves should be chopped or thinly sliced, and chives cut into about ½-inch lengths. Rosemary is a great addition too, but it gets some sauté time with the shallot to temper its stronger flavor a bit.

Grilled Clam Pouches

with Bay Leaf and Butter

Fresh bay leaves really stand out in this preparation; dried leaves won't offer as much fragrant flavor. A rosemary or thyme sprig in each packet, or a couple of fresh sage leaves, can be used in place of fresh bay. And you can't go wrong with just butter and clams on the grill either. I use 12-inch-wide aluminum foil; you can use larger and/or heavy-duty foil if you like.

The packets make a good serving vessel perched on a plate for casual dining. You can instead transfer the clams and buttery cooking juices to shallow bowls. These lighter portions are ideal as an appetizer, followed perhaps by other items destined for the grill while it's hot.

Makes 4 servings

- 2 pounds small to medium live hard-shell clams, well rinsed (see page 17)
- 4 tablespoons unsalted butter, divided
- 8 fresh bay leaves, divided
- Sliced baguette or other bread, for serving

1   Preheat an outdoor grill for medium-high direct heat.

2   Cut 8 pieces of aluminum foil about 12 inches long and arrange them on the counter stacked in pairs, for making 4 packets.

3   Put 1 tablespoon of butter in the center of each foil packet. Fold or tear each bay leaf in half, which helps release its aromatic character, and put 2 leaves on or alongside the butter for each packet. Divide the clams evenly among the pouches, mounding them on top of the butter and bay and leaving a few inches of foil around.

4   Draw the four corners of the foil up over the clams to meet in the center and crimp together along the edges, where the sides of the foil meet, so the packet →

is well sealed. The goal is to create pouches that will hold in the steam for cooking and preserve the flavorful cooking juices that result.

5   Set the foil packets on the grill, cover, and cook for about 10 to 12 minutes for small clams, 12 to 15 for medium. Partly open a packet to see if all the clams have opened, being careful to avoid the escaping steam; if not, reseal and cook for another 2 to 3 minutes.

6   Set each pouch on an individual plate and fold down the foil edges, creating a rustic bowl of sorts to hold the flavorful cooking liquids. Or carefully transfer the contents to shallow bowls. Serve right away, with bread alongside, discarding any clams that did not open.

NOTE: This recipe works well in the oven too. Preheat the oven to 475 degrees F. Use a broad, shallow vessel, such as a large cast-iron skillet or a 12-inch gratin dish or similar baking dish. Add the butter pieces and bay leaves to the dish and put in the oven until the butter has melted. Take the dish from the oven, add the clams in a relatively even layer, and return the dish to the oven. Roast until all, or mostly all, of the clams have opened, 12 to 15 minutes. Spoon the clams into individual shallow bowls, discarding any that did not open, then carefully pour the buttery cooking liquids over the top.

Stuffed Clams

with Pork Rinds

The interesting combination of clams and pork shows up in some delicious guises, such as a traditional Portuguese stew (*porco à alentejana*). And there's that bacon that often finds its way into a pot of clam chowder. Here the pork element is a bit more subtle, taking the form of crisp pork rinds that stand in for the bread crumbs sometimes used for stuffed clams. You may see a number of flavor options in the snack aisle; the traditional unflavored rinds will be best here.

Because of variances in meat-to-shell ratios of clams, the amount of chopped clams in your filling can vary as well. Adjust as needed, which could mean using less filling per shell, or filling fewer of the shells.

Makes 6 to 8 servings

- 36 medium live hard-shell clams (about 2½ pounds), well rinsed (see page 17)
- ½ cup dry white wine or water
- 2 teaspoons mild olive oil
- ½ cup finely chopped celery
- ½ cup finely chopped green onions, white and light-green parts
- ½ teaspoon minced garlic
- 1 cup finely chopped pork rinds
- Freshly ground black pepper

1 Preheat the oven to 400 degrees F.

2 Put the clams and wine in a medium pot, set the pot over medium-high heat, and cover. After 2 to 3 minutes, gently stir the clams with a large slotted spoon. Cover the pot and continue cooking, stirring once or twice more, until all, or mostly all, of the clams have opened, 2 to 5 minutes longer. Use the slotted spoon to transfer the opened clams to a large bowl. Continue cooking any remaining clams for 1 to 2 minutes, but discard any not opened after that time. If the liquids boil vigorously at any point, reduce the heat a bit. →

3 Pour the cooking liquids from the pot through a small fine-mesh sieve into a small bowl, leaving behind any grit in the bottom of the pot. When the clams are cool enough to handle, remove the meats and reserve half of each shell. Wash these shell halves and dry them well. Add the liquids from the bottom of the bowl to those from the pot. Coarsely chop the clams; you should have about ½ cup—more is even better, with less you may fill fewer shells.

4 Heat the oil in a medium skillet over medium heat. Add the celery, green onions, and garlic and cook, stirring occasionally, until tender, 2 to 3 minutes. Take the skillet from the heat and add the pork rinds, clam meats, ¼ cup of the reserved clam juice, and a few grindings of black pepper. Stir to mix and evenly incorporate the clams. The pork rinds will absorb much of the liquid, and the mixture should be moist but not soupy; if it's a bit on the dry side, add more clam juice a tablespoon at a time.

5 Spoon the clam filling into the cleaned shells (as many as you have filling for) and set them on a rimmed baking sheet. Bake the clams until the juices bubble at the edges and the tops are lightly browned, 5 to 7 minutes. Use tongs to transfer the clams to a serving platter or individual plates and serve.

Clam Puttanesca Mini Pizzas

The bold flavors of classic puttanesca pair well with sweet, briny clams; here the two are perched on pizza dough in snack-size portions. Use a favorite homemade pizza dough recipe, or look for prepared dough, which may be available frozen at your grocery store. Pull out your pizza stone, if you've got one, and use according to manufacturer's instructions. Caesar salad would be a great accompaniment.

Makes 4 servings

- About 1 pound prepared pizza dough, thawed if frozen
- 2 pounds small to medium live hard-shell clams, well rinsed (see page 17)
- ¼ cup water
- All-purpose flour, for forming dough
- 2 medium tomatoes (about 12 ounces), seeded and finely chopped (see page 74)
- ¼ cup finely chopped green olives
- 3 tablespoons finely chopped fresh flat-leaf parsley
- 2 tablespoons drained capers
- 1 anchovy fillet, finely chopped
- 1 teaspoon chopped garlic
- ⅛ teaspoon dried red pepper flakes
- 1 tablespoon mild or extra-virgin olive oil

1 Preheat the oven to 475 degrees F. Line a rimmed baking sheet with parchment paper or a silicone baking mat.

2 Cut the pizza dough into 4 equal pieces, form each into a ball, and cover with a kitchen towel to rest while cooking the clams.

3 Put the clams and water in a medium pot, set the pot over medium-high heat, and cover. After 2 to 3 minutes, gently stir the clams with a large slotted spoon. Cover the pot and continue cooking until all, or mostly all, of the clams have opened, 2 to 5 minutes longer. Use the slotted spoon to transfer the opened clams to a large bowl. Continue cooking any remaining clams for 1 to 2 minutes, but discard any not opened after that time. If the liquids boil vigorously at →

any point, reduce the heat a bit. When the clams are cool enough to handle, remove the meats.

4   Working on a lightly floured surface, flatten each round of dough with your fingers, then use a rolling pin to roll them into roughly 6–inch rounds. If the dough begins springing back quite a lot, let that piece rest while rolling out other rounds; after a few minutes it should be easier to roll out again. Lightly dust the dough with more flour as needed, but avoid overdoing it. Set the dough rounds on the prepared baking sheet, covered with a kitchen towel.

5   Combine the tomatoes, olives, parsley, capers, anchovy, garlic, and pepper flakes in a small bowl, tossing well with a fork to evenly mix. The anchovy pieces in particular tend to clump; break them up as best you can.

6   Brush each dough round with some oil, leaving about ½ inch bare around the edges. Scatter the clams over each pizza and top with the puttanesca mixture, spreading it out evenly.

7   Bake until the dough is puffed and browned on the edges and the topping is sizzling, 8 to 12 minutes. Use a spatula to transfer the pizzas to individual plates and serve.

Open-Faced Clam and Quick-Pickled Carrot Sandwiches

With inspiration from the open-faced sandwiches of Scandinavia, this recipe has an interesting blend of flavors: briny, rich, sweet, vinegary, and bright. The bread I use comes in dense rectangular slices with lots of whole grain, not a typical sandwich bread. Other similarly dense dark bread can be used. Or serve the clam-carrot mixture on a cracker-like option, such as rye crispbread, with or without the spread of butter. Note that the clams and carrots sit in the refrigerator for at least an hour before serving.

Makes 6 to 8 servings

- 1½ teaspoons caraway seeds
- ¼ cup red wine vinegar
- ¾ teaspoon kosher salt, plus more if needed
- 2 pounds small live hard-shell clams, well rinsed (see page 17)
- ¼ cup dry white wine or water
- 1 cup coarsely grated carrot (about 1 medium carrot)
- ¼ cup very thinly sliced red onion
- 2 tablespoons coarsely chopped fresh flat-leaf parsley
- 4 tablespoons salted butter, at room temperature (see note)
- 4 large slices dense pumpernickel or other dense rye bread

1 Put the caraway seeds in a small, dry skillet and toast over medium heat, stirring or gently tossing frequently, until just a bit darker in color and aromatic, 1 to 2 minutes. Transfer the seeds to a small plate or dish to avoid over-toasting and set aside to cool.

2 Combine the vinegar and salt in a medium bowl, stirring until the salt dissolves. Set aside.

3 Put the clams and wine in a medium pot, set the pot over medium-high heat, and cover. After 2 to 3 minutes, gently stir the clams with a large slotted spoon.

Cover the pot and continue cooking, stirring once or twice more, until all, or mostly all, of the clams have opened, 2 to 5 minutes longer. Use the slotted spoon to transfer the opened clams to a large bowl. Continue cooking any remaining clams for 1 to 2 minutes, but discard any not opened after that time. If the liquids boil vigorously at any point, reduce the heat a bit.

4   When the clams are cool enough to handle, remove the meats. Small clams can be used as is, otherwise coarsely chop the clams. Add the clams to the vinegar. Pour the cooking liquids from the pot through a small fine-mesh sieve into a small bowl, leaving behind any grit in the bottom of the pot. Add the liquids from the bottom of the large bowl to those from the pot.

5   Add ¼ cup of the clam cooking liquids to the clam and vinegar mixture; remaining liquids can be saved for another use (see page 22). Stir to mix, then add the carrot, onion, and 1 teaspoon of the caraway seeds, tossing gently to evenly mix. Cover and refrigerate for 1 to 2 hours.

6   Put the parsley on a cutting board and top it with the remaining ½ teaspoon of the caraway seeds, then finely chop them together. This will garnish the sandwiches.

7   Spread the butter on the bread and cut the bread into roughly 3-inch pieces—triangles, squares, or rectangles, depending on the shape of bread used.

8   Drain the clams and carrots in a fine-mesh sieve and set the sieve over a bowl to continue draining while assembling the sandwiches. Spoon some of the clam and carrot mixture onto each piece of bread, spreading it out relatively evenly. Top with a generous pinch of the parsley-caraway mixture and serve.

NOTE: For this recipe, I prefer salted butter for accentuating the flavors of the other ingredients. If you only have unsalted butter, simply stir a good pinch of kosher salt into it.

Mussels

The legendary Northwest gastronome James Beard noted in his 1972 classic *James Beard's American Cookery* that mussels "remain the most neglected of all our shellfish." It's perhaps understandable that they were overlooked for so long; those clusters of dark shells that accumulate on pier pilings and rocks are not all that appealing at first glance. Though it's a shame it took so long for mussels to become more broadly loved in the United States. All those years we could have been taking inspiration from Spanish paella and the *moules frites* (steamed mussels with fries) of Belgium.

The blue mussel is a prolific species found throughout the North Atlantic. In the United States, this mussel is harvested in the wild and farm-raised primarily in New England. The shells can be so darkly colored as to look more black than blue. On the West Coast, the transplanted Mediterranean mussel is grown by many aquaculture operations, and the native Pacific blue mussel is in limited production as well.

These three varieties of mussels are similar enough in appearance, with an elongated teardrop shape slightly angled on one side, that they can be difficult to distinguish with an untrained eye. In the kitchen, they're fully interchangeable.

Although there may be slight variations with different species and regions, mussels are generally available year-round.

Shopping and Storing

Mussels are generally sold by the pound. You may see them in bulk, so you can buy a specific amount, or in bags of a set quantity. Because mussels have thinner shells than clams, it's not uncommon to get home and find some with broken shells. Consider buying a few more mussels than needed in the recipe to account for that.

Mussels purchased in the shell are alive and need to stay alive until you cook them. If it's a hot day or your trip home from the store will be a long one, ask at the seafood counter for a bag of ice to accompany the mussels. Or plan ahead and put a cooler with some frozen gel packs in the car.

When you get home, transfer the mussels to a large bowl. I put the mussels first in a colander, then set that in the bowl so the mussels sit above any water that accumulates in the bottom of the bowl. Cover the mussels with a damp, but not sopping wet, kitchen towel to keep them moist until needed. Don't cover the bowl any more than that; the mussels need air to survive. And don't be tempted to store the mussels in water or top them with ice, as they can expire in fresh water.

Cleaning

Mussels should be cleaned just before cooking. If you see the tough, stringy byssal thread, or beard, with which mussels attach themselves to their home base, it needs to be removed. It can be a little tricky to get a good grip with bare fingers: try grabbing it using a paper towel, tugging gently to remove the beard from the mussel. For anything else attached to the shell, such as other strands of the beard or a stray barnacle, scrape them away with a scrub brush or the back of a small knife.

Rinse the debearded mussels well by tossing gently in a colander under cold running water. As you clean the mussels, discard any with broken shells. If any shells are gaping, tap the mussel on the counter: if its shell does not close firmly, discard that mussel as well.

Cooking

Cooking mussels follows pretty much the same principles, and versatility, as cooking clams. Casual, quick, easy, and with plenty of room for variation to suit your tastes. The liquid used to steam open mussels can be water, wine, beer, or hard cider. I prefer crisp, dry options, any hint of acidity a bonus. And as with any time you cook with these potable ingredients, choose something of a quality you'll want to drink alongside as well: a little for the pot, a little for you and your guests.

Beyond steaming, mussels in the shell are great roasted, grilled, sautéed, and stewed. The cooked meats have countless possibilities, from a tapas-like nibbles to pasta dishes to substantial salads with grains and vegetables.

Steamed Mussels
with Kimchi and Daikon

Steamed mussels can be exquisitely simple, with little more than a splash of wine added to the pot. But they take well to bold flavors too. The crunch of both kimchi and daikon add contrast to the tender meat as well. You may see a number of kimchi varieties available; I used the more common cabbage version for this recipe. This is great for a light supper with a salad and/or roasted vegetables alongside.

Makes 2 to 4 servings

- ¾ cup kimchi
- 4 ounces daikon radish, peeled and julienned (about 1 cup)
- ½ cup dry white wine or water
- 3 pounds live mussels, scrubbed and debearded (see page 40)
- 4 green onions, white and green portions thinly sliced
- Sliced baguette or other bread, for serving

1. Coarsely chop any larger pieces of kimchi; smaller bite-size pieces can be used as is. Put the kimchi, daikon, and wine in a medium pot and add the mussels. Set the pot over medium-high heat and cover. After 2 to 3 minutes, gently stir the mussels with a large slotted spoon. Cover the pot and continue cooking, stirring once or twice more, until all, or mostly all, of the mussels have opened, 2 to 4 minutes longer.

2. Scoop the mussels into shallow bowls, discarding any that did not open, and distribute the kimchi, daikon, and cooking liquids evenly among the bowls, leaving any grit behind in the pot. Scatter the green onion over and serve right away with bread alongside.

Mussels

with Mustard and Mustard Greens

This slight variation on the steaming technique cooks mussels in a pot with a bit of liquid, but does so without adding the lid. You can use other braising greens if you like, but stick to those that will wilt quickly, such as spinach, baby kale, or chard. To round out a dinner, serve the mussels with fried or roasted potatoes.

Makes 2 to 4 servings

- 3 tablespoons unsalted butter
- ½ cup finely chopped shallot or yellow onion
- ½ cup dry white wine or water
- 2 tablespoons Dijon mustard
- ¼ teaspoon kosher salt

- Freshly ground black pepper
- 3 pounds live mussels, scrubbed and debearded (see page 40)
- 4 cups loosely packed mustard greens, tough stems removed and larger leaves torn

1 Melt the butter in a medium pot over medium heat. Add the shallot and cook, stirring, until tender and aromatic, 2 to 3 minutes. Stir in the wine, mustard, salt, and a few grindings of black pepper, then add the mussels. Increase the heat to medium-high and cook, stirring often, until all, or mostly all, of the mussels have opened, 5 to 8 minutes.

2 Add the greens to the pot and stir gently into the mussels so the greens wilt, 1 to 2 minutes. Scoop the mussels and greens into shallow bowls, discarding any mussels that did not open. Pour the cooking liquids over the mussels, leaving any grit behind in the pot, and serve right away.

Mussel Stew

with Winter Squash and Green Curry

The earthy sweetness of winter squash is a great complement to mussels, and their vivid color is striking against the dark shells in this quick stew inspired by flavors of Southeast Asia. Delicata squash is a favorite for its small size and skin thin enough to not require peeling. Other winter squash can be used, their thicker skin peeled before using.

Makes 4 servings

- About 1 pound delicata, butternut, or kabocha squash
- 2 tablespoons mild olive oil
- 1 large or 2 small leeks, trimmed, cleaned (see sidebar), and cut into ¼-inch slices (about 1½ cups)
- 2 medium carrots, cut into ¼-inch slices (about 1 cup)
- 2 tablespoons green curry paste
- 1½ cups Shellfish Stock (page 183) or clam juice (see page 22)
- ½ cup full-fat or lite canned coconut milk
- ¼ teaspoon kosher salt
- 2½ pounds live mussels, scrubbed and debearded (see page 40)
- Chopped fresh cilantro or flat-leaf parsley, for serving

1 Cut the delicata in half lengthwise and scoop out the seeds. Halve each piece lengthwise again, then cut across into ¾-inch slices. Other winter squash should be peeled and seeded, then cut into about ¾-inch cubes.

2 Heat the oil in a medium pot over medium heat. Add the leek and carrots and cook, stirring occasionally, until the leek is tender, 3 to 4 minutes. Add the curry paste and cook for 1 minute, stirring constantly to evenly coat the vegetables. Stir in the stock, coconut milk, and salt, then add the squash. Stir to incorporate and bring just to a low boil, then cover and simmer over medium-low heat until the squash is nearly tender (less firm than when raw but the tip of a knife still meets some resistance), about 5 to 10 minutes depending on the type used. →

3   Add the mussels and increase the heat to medium-high. Cook uncovered, stirring occasionally and gently until all, or mostly all, of the mussels have opened, 5 to 8 minutes.

4   Scoop the stew into shallow bowls, discarding any mussels that did not open. Sprinkle with cilantro, and serve right away.

CLEANING LEEKS

Leeks can often harbor dirt, so it's best to clean them before using. First trim away the root end and the darker-green top portion, which is tough (though after rinsing, the tops can be added to a batch of Shellfish Stock on page 183). Then cut the leek in half lengthwise and run cool water through the layers to draw off any dirt. Dry well with a kitchen towel.

Mussels Roasted

with Potatoes and Chiles

When they're available, small fingerling potatoes are perfect for this recipe. Otherwise small red or white potatoes work well, cut into smaller pieces as needed for even cooking. To temper the heat of the chiles, you can remove the seeds from the slices. You can also use a milder chile instead, such as Anaheim. This can be served in small portions as a sort of tapas offering with drinks, or for two as a main course with sautéed zucchini or another green vegetable alongside.

Makes 2 main-course or 6 appetizer servings

- 12 ounces fingerling or other small potatoes, scrubbed
- 2 to 3 medium jalapeños, trimmed and cut into ¼-inch slices (seeded if you like)
- 2 tablespoons mild olive oil
- ¼ teaspoon kosher salt
- Freshly ground black pepper
- 2½ pounds live mussels, scrubbed and debearded (see page 40)

1 Preheat the oven to 475 degrees F.

2 Depending on the size and shape of the potatoes you're using, cut them into pieces as needed: larger fingerlings in half lengthwise and/or across into pieces about 1½ inches long; round potatoes in half or quarters. Small fingerlings or little "nugget" potatoes can be cooked as is.

3 Put the potatoes in a steamer rack in a medium saucepan set above a couple of inches of water. Cover, bring the water to a boil, and steam until the potatoes are about half cooked: a paring knife should pierce with a little resistance, 7 to 10 minutes. Remove the potatoes from the steamer and set aside to cool and dry.

4 Combine the potatoes and jalapeño slices in a 9-by-13-inch baking dish and drizzle the oil over, then add the salt and a few grindings of black pepper. Gently toss well so the vegetables are evenly coated in oil. Spread them in a →

relatively even layer and roast until the potatoes are partly browned and the jalapeños are mostly tender, 10 to 12 minutes.

5   Remove the baking dish from the oven and add the mussels in a relatively even layer. Return the baking dish to the oven and roast until the mussels have opened, 6 to 8 minutes.

6   Scoop the mussels (discarding any that did not open), potatoes, and jalapeños into shallow bowls, spoon the cooking liquids over, and serve right away.

Crostini with Mussels

in Romesco Sauce

Romesco is a versatile sauce with roasted pepper, tomato, almonds, garlic, and a little chile heat that pairs well with seafood. Here, steamed mussels are tossed in a quick version of the sauce and used as a topping for toasted baguette. Other sliced bread can be used as well, cut into pieces easy enough to manage in a couple of bites.

The red pepper and tomato can be pretty wet after roasting, so I dry them before continuing to avoid a watery sauce. If, after sitting, the sauce has excess liquid collecting at the edges, you can drain it off before serving.

Makes 6 to 8 servings

- 1 medium red bell pepper
- 1 small tomato (about 5 ounces), halved
- ⅓ cup slivered almonds, toasted
- 2 tablespoons sherry vinegar or red wine vinegar, plus more to taste
- 1½ teaspoons chopped garlic
- ¼ teaspoon kosher salt
- ¼ teaspoon dried red pepper flakes
- 24 slices baguette or similar-size bread slices
- 1 to 2 tablespoons mild olive oil
- 2 pounds live mussels, scrubbed and debearded (see page 40)
- ¼ cup water
- 2 teaspoons fresh thyme or oregano leaves

1 Preheat the broiler and set the oven rack 5 to 6 inches below the element.

2 Put the whole bell pepper and tomato halves (cut side down) on a rimmed baking sheet lined with aluminum foil and broil, turning the pepper occasionally (the tomato halves just stay as is), until the pepper is tender and the skin blackens, 12 to 15 minutes. Put the pepper in a bowl and cover securely with plastic wrap. Transfer the tomato halves to a small plate; set both aside to cool. Set the oven temperature to 400 degrees F and return the oven rack to the center.

3   When the pepper is cool, peel away and discard the skin, then remove the core and seeds. When the tomato is cool, peel away and discard the skin, then scoop out and discard the seeds. Dry both with a paper towel to draw off excess liquid, then chop the pepper and tomato and put them in a food processor. Add the almonds, vinegar, garlic, salt, and pepper flakes and pulse until finely chopped and well blended but not quite a smooth purée; I like to leave a little texture to this sauce. Taste for seasoning, adding more salt if needed. Transfer the romesco to a medium serving bowl and set aside.

4   Lightly brush one side of each baguette slice with some of the oil and arrange the slices on a rimmed baking sheet. Bake until lightly toasted, 3 to 5 minutes. Transfer to a wire rack to cool.

5   Put the mussels and water in a medium pot, set the pot over medium-high heat, and cover. After 2 to 3 minutes, gently stir the mussels with a large slotted spoon. Cover the pot and continue cooking, stirring once or twice more, until all, or mostly all, of the mussels have opened, 2 to 4 minutes longer. Use the slotted spoon to transfer the opened mussels to a large bowl. Continue cooking any remaining mussels for 1 to 2 minutes, but discard any not opened after that time. If the liquids boil vigorously at any point, reduce the heat a bit.

6   When the mussels are cool enough to handle, remove the meats and scatter them on paper towels to drain. Add the mussels and thyme to the romesco sauce and stir to evenly mix. Serve with the toasted bread alongside, each guest topping their own crostini with a mussel or two and a bit of sauce.

Mussel and Chickpea Salad

Flavorful and hearty, this salad can stand alone as a light meal or serve with warmed pita bread and tzatziki. It can be made a day ahead and refrigerated; the flavor will be best if it sits at room temperature a bit before serving, stirred well to reincorporate the dressing that settles to the bottom of the bowl. The salad could also travel well for a picnic, kept cold en route.

Makes 4 to 6 servings

- 3 tablespoons red wine vinegar
- ¼ teaspoon kosher salt
- Freshly ground black pepper
- ⅓ cup extra-virgin or mild olive oil
- 3 tablespoons finely chopped fresh flat-leaf parsley, basil, and/or chives
- 2 pounds live mussels, scrubbed and debearded (see page 40)
- ¼ cup water

- 1 (15-ounce) can chickpeas, rinsed and well drained
- 1 medium zucchini, diced (about 1½ cups)
- 1 cup moderately packed thinly sliced spinach (about 1 ounce)
- ½ cup crumbled feta cheese (about 2 ounces)
- ¼ cup slivered sun-dried tomato, oil-packed or rehydrated dry

1   Whisk together the vinegar and salt with a couple of grindings of black pepper in a large bowl until the salt is dissolved. Whisk in the oil, then add the herbs. Set the dressing aside.

2   Put the mussels and water in a medium pot, set the pot over medium-high heat, and cover. After 2 to 3 minutes, gently stir the mussels with a large slotted spoon. Cover the pot and continue cooking, stirring once or twice more, until all, or mostly all, of the mussels have opened, 2 to 5 minutes longer. Use the slotted spoon to transfer the opened mussels to a large bowl. Continue cooking any remaining mussels for 1 to 2 minutes, but discard any not opened after that time. If the liquids boil vigorously at any point, reduce the heat a bit.

3   When the mussels have cooled, remove the meats and add them to the bowl with the dressing. Add the chickpeas, zucchini, spinach, feta, and sun-dried

tomato and toss gently to evenly mix and coat with the dressing. Taste for seasoning, adding more salt or pepper to taste.

4   Spoon the salad into individual bowls and serve right away. Or cover the salad and refrigerate until ready to serve, up to a day later, letting it sit at room temperature for 15 to 20 minutes before serving.

Pan-Fried Mussel and Sage Bites

A perfect snack for your next cocktail party or game-night gathering, this isn't a complicated recipe but it does take a bit of time—mussels are steamed and the meats tossed in seasoned flour to pan-fry. You can steam the mussels, store them in their cooking liquids in the refrigerator, and make the seasoned flour an hour or two ahead. Then finish things off just before serving. Fancy picks that have a frilly top or other fun accent are great, or simple round toothpicks work just as well. This recipe has larger mussels in mind, though you may not have a choice when shopping. Smaller mussels may need more flour to thoroughly coat them, and you might want to get more than twenty-four.

Makes 4 to 6 servings

- 5 tablespoons mild olive oil, divided, plus more if needed
- 24 medium fresh sage leaves (see note) plus 2 teaspoons finely chopped fresh sage
- 24 large live mussels (about 1½ pounds), scrubbed and debearded (see page 40)
- ¼ cup water
- 1 medium lemon
- 4 tablespoons all-purpose flour, divided, plus more if needed
- ½ teaspoon kosher salt
- Freshly ground black pepper

1   Heat 2 tablespoons of the oil in a small skillet over medium heat. Add the sage leaves and cook until just lightly crisp, stirring occasionally with a fork to ensure they cook evenly, 1 to 2 minutes; they shouldn't brown much. With the fork, lift out the leaves to a paper towel to drain. When just cool enough to handle, pierce each leaf onto a small serving pick about ¾ inch from the end; fully cooled crisp leaves are harder to pierce without breaking.

2   Put the mussels and water in a medium pot, set the pot over medium-high heat, and cover. After 2 to 3 minutes, gently stir the mussels with a large slotted →

spoon. Cover the pot and continue cooking, stirring once or twice more, until all, or mostly all, of the mussels have opened, 2 to 4 minutes longer. Use the slotted spoon to transfer the opened mussels to a large bowl. Continue cooking any remaining mussels for 1 to 2 minutes, but discard any not opened after that time. If the liquids boil vigorously at any point, reduce the heat a bit.

3 Pour the cooking liquids from the pot through a small fine-mesh sieve into a medium bowl, leaving behind any grit in the bottom of the pot. When the mussels are cool enough to handle, remove the meats and put them in the bowl with the cooking liquids.

4 Finely grate enough zest from the lemon to measure 2 teaspoons. Cut the lemon into 8 wedges and set aside for serving.

5 Combine 3 tablespoons of the flour, the lemon zest, finely chopped sage, salt, and a few grindings of pepper in a mini processor and pulse for about a minute to incorporate the zest and sage well with the flour. Put the flour in a large bowl. (If you don't have a mini processor, just stir them all together well in a large bowl, carefully breaking up any clusters of the zest.)

6 Drain the mussels in a sieve and add them still damp to the flour, tossing with a fork to quickly and evenly coat in the flour. Add the remaining tablespoon of flour and toss to coat. If the mussels become a little sticky while sitting, add another tablespoon or so of flour and toss. Too much extra flour diminishes the lemon-sage flavors; the goal is just enough to keep the mussels from sticking to each other, and flouring them in stages helps ensure an even coating.

7 Heat a medium heavy skillet, preferably cast iron, over medium heat. When hot, add the remaining 3 tablespoons oil and heat for a few moments. Add about half of the mussels (less if necessary to avoid crowding), gently shaking off any excess flour if needed. Spread them out evenly and cook until nicely browned on one side, about 2 minutes. Turn and brown well on the second side. Scoop out to a plate and repeat with the remaining mussels, adding more oil to the skillet if needed.

8 Arrange the mussels on a serving plate and pierce each with a sage-leaf-studded pick—ideally the sage leaf will be resting on the surface of the mussel. Arrange the lemon wedges around for squeezing, and serve right away.

NOTE: Don't fret if you don't have enough sage leaves for every mussel, you can either cut larger leaves in half, or include the leaves on half the mussels instead of all of them. The mussels are delicious without that crisp embellishment on top, so you can skip the fried sage leaf garnish as well.

Scallops

One of the most interesting things about scallops—to me, at least—is that they are so mobile relative to their fellow bivalves. In their natural states, oysters sit rather still on a beach, clams burrow into sand, and mussels cling to rocks and pilings. But not scallops. They live free, scooting around the sea floor, locomoting with the opening and closing of their shells. (Apparently, while young, they're quite the impressive swimmers, and become a bit less mobile as they get older.) The adductor muscle that facilitates the shell action is the same thing that we sever in an oyster to remove it from its shell. The scallop's version is much larger relative to that of other bivalves, and is usually the only part of the scallop that we eat.

The Atlantic sea scallop is the most abundant variety available in the United States. They are generally found from Maine as far south as North Carolina, though most of the harvest comes from Massachusetts. Alaska waters are home to the weathervane scallop, which is harvested in smaller volumes than are the Atlantic scallops. Weathervane scallops are available in the same range of sizes as are Atlantic sea scallops and can be used interchangeably for them in recipes.

The smaller bay scallop is found in roughly the same area as the Atlantic sea scallop, though at harvest levels that are a small fraction of those for sea scallops. Nantucket bay scallops are a treat to enjoy when possible.

Among other scallops that are worth enjoying when available are the small pink, or "singing," scallops from the Pacific

Northwest, so named because of their pretty pink shells and someone's interpretation that the shells opening and closing made it look as though they were singing their way through the water. These are small and often cooked and served in their shells, akin to clams or mussels.

Scallops are mostly a wild product, at least in terms of the domestic supply. Fishing for Atlantic sea scallops occurs throughout the year, with peak harvest usually spring into early summer, available fresh and frozen. Alaska weathervane scallops are fished primarily in summer, with most of the catch frozen at sea, offering consistent availability through the year. Bay scallops have a limited season over the winter months in the United States, with frozen bay scallops available year round.

Shopping and Storing

Most sea scallops are shucked at sea; just the luscious meat comes to shore. You won't often see a sea scallop sold in its shell, though on occasion in specialty markets.

Scallops are generally white in color, but there are natural variances that can include ivory, light beige, and even pale orange. The aroma should be fresh and clean, no hints of ammonia or other sharp or sour smells.

Scallops should look moist and glisten. While dry-pack scallops have less moisture than other scallops, no scallop should look dried out. Frozen scallops should not have any exposed, dry-looking patches, which can indicate freezer burn.

"Dry-pack" may not be the most evocative of descriptions, but is a characteristic worth seeking out when buying scallops. This "dry" indicates that the scallops were not treated with sodium tripolyphosphate, an additive that helps scallops retain moisture.

The benefit of using dry-pack scallops is that they will give off a minimum amount of water, if any, during cooking. Extra water impedes the browning of a good sear in the skillet and can dilute sauces and otherwise alter the intended outcome of a recipe. When it's particularly advantageous to use dry-pack scallops, I've noted this in the recipe. If not using dry-pack scallops, take extra care to dry them well before cooking to minimize excess liquid.

Sea scallops and weathervane scallops are frequently sold with a size indication of some kind. It may be general, such as "medium" or "jumbo." Or it may echo industry-standard size grading, such as "U-10" or "30/40," referencing how many scallops (on average) will be in one pound: under 10 for the former, and 30 to 40 for the latter. It's the same idea behind the size grades often listed for shrimp; the larger the number, the smaller the scallop.

Fresh scallops should be stored, well wrapped, in the refrigerator. As long as the packaging they came home in is in good shape, just store them as is. It should be okay to hold them a day before cooking, but the sooner you cook them the better they'll be—my usual mantra with all shellfish. If you bought still-frozen scallops, get them in the freezer right away to avoid any premature thaw. Don't try to refreeze a scallop that has thawed.

Cleaning

There may be a little side muscle at the edge of your scallops (if not removed during processing), a tough piece that should be removed before cooking. It peels away easily with your fingers. Otherwise scallops don't generally need cleaning before use, only the briefest of rinses under cold water. Just ensure that scallops are well dried before cooking, particularly before searing or pan-frying.

Cooking

This is one shellfish in this collection that you'll rarely see sold in its shell, so recipes here use just the shucked meat. Still, scallops are quite versatile.

The simplest way to experience the best a large scallop has to offer is a quick sear in a hot skillet until richly browned on each side, just a matter of minutes. You'll see here a couple of recipes with seared scallops, plus others that serve them raw, baked, sautéed, and grilled. It's always good to avoid overcooking shellfish, and with scallops it's a bit more imperative as they become rubbery and less flavorful if cooked too long.

For many recipes, any size of scallop can be used, keeping in mind that smaller scallops will cook more quickly. Bay scallops and smaller sea and weathervane scallops are ideal in sautés, soups, pastas, salads, and similar dishes mixed with other ingredients. Big scallops—those weighing an ounce or more each— are perfect for the elegant presentation of a seared scallop. And they're ideal for the grill too, with less risk of overcooking.

Sautéed Scallops

with Ginger-Rosé Sauce

Simple sautés like this are often finished with a splash of white wine, but for this one I grabbed a bottle of rosé instead. Rosé wines can range from bone dry to rather fruity. I recommend one toward the dry end, perfect to sip alongside as well. This is a great recipe for bay scallops or smaller sea scallops. If you use larger sea scallops, add a minute or two more cooking time, depending on how large they are. In place of rice, the scallops could be served with sautéed greens.

Makes 4 servings

- 1 to 1½ pounds bay scallops or small sea scallops
- 5 tablespoons unsalted butter, divided
- 6 green onions, white and light-green portions cut into ½-inch pieces on the bias

- 2 tablespoons julienned fresh ginger (from about a 1-inch piece of peeled ginger)
- ⅓ cup dry rosé wine
- ¼ teaspoon kosher salt
- Cooked jasmine rice or other long grain rice, for serving

1   Remove and discard the tough little side muscle if it's present on any of the scallops. Drain the scallops on paper towels, with a piece of paper towel pressed on top if they're particularly wet; set aside.

2   Cut 3 tablespoons of the butter into 3 to 4 pieces and put it in the refrigerator to chill.

3   Melt the remaining 2 tablespoons butter in a large skillet over medium heat. Add the scallops and cook, stirring occasionally, until evenly opaque on the surface and just a touch of translucence remains at the center when cut into, 3 to 5 minutes. Use a slotted spoon to scoop the scallops onto a plate and set aside.

4   Add the green onions and ginger to the skillet and cook, stirring often, until tender and aromatic, 2 to 3 minutes. Add the rosé and increase the heat to

medium-high, simmering the liquid until reduced by about half and stirring to lift up flavorful bits stuck to the bottom of the skillet, 2 to 3 minutes.

5   Take the skillet from the heat and add the chilled butter, stirring or swirling gently so the butter melts creamily into the pan liquids, creating a simple sauce. Set the skillet over low heat, add the scallops and salt, and warm gently, stirring, for about 1 minute. Taste for seasoning, adding more salt if needed.

6   Spoon the scallops and sauce over rice on individual plates, and serve right away.

Sea Scallops

with Apple–Celery Root Slaw

Celery root, also known as celeriac, has hints of the more common celery stalks' flavor, though with added earthiness and firmer texture. Extra can be used as you might other root vegetables: roasted, in a soup, paired with potatoes in a gratin. If you're unable to find celery root, a few tender inner stalks of celery, thinly sliced, can be used instead. To get the best sear on these scallops, try to find dry-pack scallops. An arugula salad would be a great accompaniment.

Makes 4 servings

- 1 to 1¼ pounds large sea scallops
- 1 tablespoon mild olive oil

  ───────────

  For the apple-celery root slaw
- 3 tablespoons extra-virgin olive oil
- 2 tablespoons cider vinegar
- 2 teaspoons Dijon mustard

- ¼ teaspoon kosher salt
- Freshly ground black pepper
- 1 small tart apple (about 6 ounces), cored and julienned
- ¼ trimmed celery root (about 4 ounces), julienned (see note)

1   Remove and discard the tough little side muscle if it's present on any of the scallops. Drain the scallops on paper towels, with a piece of paper towel pressed on top if they're particularly wet; set aside.

2   For the slaw, combine the extra-virgin olive oil, vinegar, mustard, salt, and a few grindings of pepper in a medium bowl and mix with a fork until well blended. Spoon 2 tablespoons into a small dish and set aside for drizzling at the end.

3   Add the apple and celery root to the bowl with the remaining dressing and toss lightly to evenly mix. Arrange the slaw in an even layer in the center of individual plates and set aside while cooking the scallops.

4   Heat a large heavy skillet (cast iron is ideal) over medium-high heat. Season the scallops lightly with salt and pepper.

5   Working quickly but carefully, add the mild olive oil to the skillet and gently swirl to coat the bottom. Use tongs to add the scallops and cook undisturbed until well browned, 1½ to 2 minutes. Turn the scallops and cook until browned on the second side, about 2 minutes longer; they should be a bit translucent at the center.

6   Arrange the scallops on top of the slaw, drizzle the reserved dressing over them, and serve right away.

NOTE: If you've never cooked with celery root, it may look daunting. Unlike turnips or carrots that have a relatively thin, smooth skin to peel away, that of celery root is thicker and often embedded with fine little root ends.

Using a chef's knife rather than a peeler, start by cutting away the top end, where you may see remnants of the stalks. Set the root then on its side and carefully cut away the rooty bits from the other bulbous end of the root, which will probably take a number of cuts at various angles, until you have a relatively even rounded surface of the off-white flesh exposed around that base. (To make quicker work of this, you can simply lop off a larger piece of the base to remove all that rooty stuff at once, but I find that cuts away too much flesh with it.) Now set the root with the flat top side down on the cutting board and use the knife to cut away the skin remaining around the sides of the celery root.

Grilled Sea Scallops and Radicchio

with Caesar Sauce

This is an ideal recipe for large sea or weathervane scallops, a bit less worry about overcooking on the hot grill. The slight bitterness of radicchio—which is tempered a bit with cooking—is a delicious complement to their sweet flavor. Since the scallops and radicchio don't need much grilling time, consider having other things, such as vegetables or flatbread, ready to grill for serving alongside. If the radicchio heads you find are small, you can use two and cut each in quarters, rather than eighths. For the Parmesan shavings, use a vegetable peeler to shave long thin strips of the cheese.

Makes 4 servings

For the Caesar sauce
- ¼ cup freshly grated Parmesan cheese
- 2 cloves garlic, chopped
- ¼ cup freshly squeezed lemon juice (from about 2 small lemons), plus more to taste
- ¼ cup mayonnaise
- 2 anchovy fillets, chopped
- ¼ teaspoon Worcestershire sauce
- ¼ cup mild olive oil

- Freshly ground black pepper

  ———————

- 16 large sea scallops (about 1 pound)
- 1 large head radicchio (about 12 ounces)
- 3 tablespoons mild olive oil, divided, plus more if needed
- Kosher salt and freshly ground black pepper
- Parmesan shavings, for serving

1   If using bamboo skewers, soak eight 8- to 10-inch bamboo skewers in cold water for at least 20 minutes to limit charring on the grill.

2   To make the Caesar sauce, combine the Parmesan and garlic in a food processor (a mini processor is ideal) and pulse a few times to more finely mince and blend. Add the lemon juice, mayonnaise, anchovy, and Worcestershire sauce and blend until smooth, scraping down the sides a couple of times. →

Add the oil and a few grindings of black pepper and process again until smooth and well blended. Taste for seasoning, adding more lemon juice to taste (salt is likely not needed, but add to your taste). Transfer the dressing to a small bowl and set aside (the dressing can be made a few hours ahead and stored, covered, in the refrigerator).

3   Remove and discard the tough little side muscle if it's present on any of the scallops. Drain the scallops on paper towels, with a piece of paper towel pressed on top if they're particularly wet; set aside.

4   Preheat an outdoor grill for direct medium-high heat.

5   Peel away and discard any torn or blemished outer leaves from the radicchio. Cut the head in half through the midpoint of the core to help hold the layers of leaves together. Cut each half into 4 wedges, also cutting through the core.

6   Set the radicchio wedges on a plate or tray and brush 2 tablespoons of the oil over them, on both sides. Sprinkle them lightly with salt and pepper.

7   Thread the scallops onto the skewers, 4 at a time (see note). Brush the scallops with the remaining tablespoon olive oil and lightly season with salt and pepper.

8   Grill the radicchio wedges until nicely browned and tender, 1 to 2 minutes per side (turn more often, if needed, to avoid too much char; a bit on the edges is fine). Remove the radicchio and grill the scallops until lightly browned and just a bit translucent at the center, about 2 minutes per side.

9   Arrange the radicchio wedges on individual plates, lean the skewers of scallops on top (or remove scallops from skewers and place on the radicchio), and drizzle generously with the Caesar sauce. Scatter Parmesan shavings over and serve right away.

NOTE: Scallops on a single skewer tend to spin around when you try to maneuver them, making it tricky to turn them over on the grill. Threading 2 bamboo skewers through the scallops, one either side of center, holds them securely for turning. Line up the 4 scallops for each portion and thread the skewers through them at the same time.

Avocado with Scallop Salsa

This idea started as a good homemade salsa made fabulous by adding scallops—upgrading your basic chips-and-salsa option for happy hour. The salsa—much like a ceviche—tops avocado for a knife-and-fork option, with the chips on the side. As an alternative, you could dice the avocado to add to the scallops for a more classic chips-and-salsa scenario. Note that while the citrus juice alters the scallops flesh, making it opaque and a bit firmer after sitting, these scallops remain raw.

Makes 4 servings

- 4 ounces sea scallops or bay scallops
- ¼ cup freshly squeezed lime juice (from about 2 medium limes)
- ½ cup finely diced and seeded tomato (see sidebar)
- ¼ cup finely diced sweet onion
- 2 tablespoons finely chopped fresh cilantro or flat-leaf parsley
- 1 tablespoon minced jalapeño
- ¼ teaspoon Tabasco or other hot sauce, plus more to taste
- ¼ teaspoon kosher salt
- 2 ripe avocados, halved, pitted, and peeled
- Tortilla chips, for serving (optional)

1 Remove and discard the tough little side muscle if it's present on any of the scallops. Cut the scallops into roughly ½-inch dice. Combine the scallops and lime juice in a small bowl, stir, and refrigerate for 30 minutes.

2 Toss together the tomato, onion, cilantro, jalapeño, Tabasco, and salt in a medium bowl. Use a slotted spoon to scoop the scallop pieces from the lime juice and add them to the bowl with the tomato mixture. Toss gently to mix, and taste for seasoning, adding more Tabasco or salt if needed. You can drizzle in a tablespoon or so of the lime juice for extra flavor, but avoid making the mixture too wet.

3 Set each avocado half cut side up on an individual plate and spoon the scallop salsa into the cavity where the pit was; it's fine if some spills onto the plate. Serve with chips alongside. →

SEEDING TOMATOES

This is a step I only bother with when excess moisture from tomatoes might make a dish too wet. Set the tomato upright on a cutting board and cut the thicker outer shell of flesh away from the core in broad strips following the curve of the tomato. If any bits of seed cling to those strips of flesh, they're easy to scrape off. The strips can then be diced or julienned as needed. The remaining core can be used in a tomato sauce, soup, or other preparation.

Seared Scallops

with Capers and Lemon

This quick recipe is perfect for a celebratory dinner for two. It's an ideal time to seek out luxuriously large scallops, and dry-pack scallops help ensure getting a good sear. I also recommend warming the plates to hold the warmth of the scallops while the pan sauce is finished. As a light main course, serve them with pasta or a potato gratin alongside. For a multicourse dinner, you can serve just one or two scallops per serving.

Makes 2 main-course or 4 to 8 appetizer servings

- 8 large sea scallops (1 to 1½ ounces each)
- Kosher salt and freshly ground black pepper
- 1 tablespoon mild olive oil

- 2 tablespoons unsalted butter
- ¼ cup freshly squeezed lemon juice (from about 2 small lemons)
- 2 tablespoons capers (preferably smaller nonpareil), drained

1   Remove and discard the tough little side muscle if it's present on any of the scallops. Drain the scallops on paper towels, with a piece of paper towel pressed on top if they're particularly wet; set aside.

2   Heat a large heavy skillet (cast iron is ideal) over medium-high heat. Season the scallops lightly with salt and pepper.

3   Working quickly but carefully, add the oil to the skillet and gently swirl to coat the bottom. Use tongs to add the scallops and cook undisturbed until well browned, 1½ to 2 minutes. Turn the scallops and cook until browned on the second side, about 2 minutes longer; they should be a bit translucent at the center. Transfer the scallops immediately to warmed plates to avoid overcooking from sitting in the hot skillet any longer than needed.

4   Reduce the heat to medium, add the butter to the skillet, and stir a bit with the tongs to help it melt quickly. Add the lemon juice and capers and cook just until the lemon juice has reduced a bit, stirring to lift up cooked bits from the bottom of the skillet, about 1 minute. Spoon the sauce over the scallops and serve right away.

Bay Scallop Salad

with Citrus and Radishes

In this salad, citrus segments are tossed with crisp, peppery radishes and topped with warm scallops and a simple dressing that's assembled right in the skillet. I like the brisk flavor of the lime segments contrasting with the sweeter fruits and scallops, but if that sounds too tart to you, feel free to use a bit more orange or grapefruit, or simply leave the lime out. This is an ideal lunchtime option, served with sliced baguette, or a first course for a dinner party. Serving two at dinner, consider adding a light pasta or roasted cauliflower alongside.

Makes 2 to 4 servings

- 12 ounces bay scallops or small sea scallops
- 1 small grapefruit
- 1 small navel orange
- 1 small lime
- 1 cup thinly sliced radishes (about half a large bunch)
- 1 tablespoon mild olive oil
- 2 tablespoons extra-virgin olive oil, or more mild olive oil
- ½ teaspoon kosher salt
- Freshly ground black pepper
- 1 tablespoon chopped fresh chives, or ½ cup coarsely chopped arugula, for serving

1   Remove and discard the tough little side muscle if it's present on any of the scallops. Drain the scallops on paper towels, with a piece of paper towel pressed on top if they're particularly wet; set aside.

2   Cut the segments from the grapefruit, orange, and lime (see sidebar), collecting them together in a medium bowl. Strain the juice from the segments and set aside, and return the segments to the same bowl. If any segments are quite large, you can break them in half. Add the radishes to the citrus segments and toss gently to mix. Arrange the salad on individual plates, leaving excess juice behind in the bowl so the salads aren't too wet. Spread the salad out a bit as a bed for the scallops.

3　Heat the mild olive oil in a medium skillet over medium heat. Add the scallops and cook, stirring occasionally, until evenly opaque on the surface and just a touch of translucence remains at the center, 3 to 5 minutes. Take the skillet from the heat and use a slotted spoon to scoop the scallops onto the citrus salad on the plates.

4　Add 3 tablespoons of the reserved citrus juice, the extra-virgin olive oil, salt, and a couple of grindings of black pepper to the skillet. Warm over medium-low heat and stir to evenly blend and incorporate the flavorful bits stuck to the bottom of the skillet, 1 to 2 minutes; the dressing will reduce a bit too. Drizzle this over the scallops and citrus, scatter the chives over, and serve right away.

SEGMENTING CITRUS FRUIT

To segment citrus fruits, use a paring knife or small serrated knife to cut both ends from the fruit, just to the flesh. Set the fruit upright on a cutting board and use the knife to cut away the peel and pith (the white part under the peel), following the curve of the fruit. Try not to cut away too much of the flesh with the peel.

Working over a medium bowl to catch the juice, hold the peeled fruit in your hand and carefully slide the knife blade down one side of a section, separating it from the membrane. Cut down the other side of the same section and let it fall into the bowl. (Pick out and discard any seeds as you go.) Continue for the remaining sections, turning back the flaps of the membrane like the pages of a book. Squeeze the juice from the membrane core into the bowl and discard the core.

Scallops Baked

with Rice and Green Olives

If you don't already have a tin of smoked paprika on your shelf, you'll enjoy adding it to the mix of your spice collection. With just a few shakes, it adds earthy-robust flavor—with some heat, if you choose the hot version—to anything from toasted nuts to roasted chicken. Here it adds its character to a Spanish-influenced blend of bell pepper, almonds, green olives, and rice baked with scallops. I think the smaller-size scallops work better here, but you can use large sea scallops if you like, adding a couple of minutes of cooking time. Serve with sautéed garlicky green beans or another favorite green vegetable.

Makes 4 servings

- 1 pound bay scallops or small sea scallops
- 3 tablespoons mild olive oil, divided, plus more for the dish
- ¼ cup finely chopped yellow onion
- ½ cup long grain white rice
- ¾ teaspoon kosher salt, divided
- 1 cup Shellfish Stock (page 183), fish stock, or water
- 1 cup (about 3 ounces) pitted green olives, halved lengthwise
- ½ cup diced red bell pepper
- ¼ cup slivered almonds, toasted
- 1 teaspoon smoked paprika, sweet or hot
- Lemon wedges, for serving

1   Remove and discard the tough little side muscle if it's present on any of the scallops. Drain the scallops on paper towels, with a piece of paper towel pressed on top if they're particularly wet; set aside.

2   Preheat the oven to 425 degrees F. Lightly oil a 12–inch gratin dish or similar shallow baking dish.

3   Heat 1 tablespoon of the oil in a small skillet over medium heat. Add the onion and cook, stirring occasionally, until tender, 2 to 3 minutes. Stir in the rice and

½ teaspoon of the salt and cook, stirring, until the rice smells lightly toasty, 2 to 3 minutes.

4   Transfer the rice to the gratin dish, add the stock, and spread the rice out relatively evenly. Cover the dish with aluminum foil and bake until the liquid is absorbed and the rice is nearly tender, 15 to 18 minutes.

5   While the rice is cooking, combine the scallops, olives, bell pepper, almonds, paprika, remaining 2 tablespoons oil, and remaining ¼ teaspoon salt in a medium bowl. Use a rubber spatula to stir and mix them together well.

6   When the rice is ready, remove the dish from the oven (leaving the oven on) and carefully remove the foil, avoiding the steam that escapes. Add the scallop mixture to the rice, scraping out the seasoned oil from the bowl as well, and gently mix with the rice, then spread things out relatively evenly. Return the dish to the oven, uncovered, and bake until the scallops are just barely cooked through (only slightly translucent at the center when cut into), 8 to 10 minutes for bay scallops, 10 to 12 minutes for small sea scallops.

7   Scoop the scallops and rice onto individual plates and serve right away, with lemon wedges alongside for squeezing.

Oysters

Every one of these shellfish has its charms, its history, its fan base of devotees that eagerly extol its virtues. But by my estimation, oysters manage to draw the most boisterous enthusiasm. The explosion of oysters bars across the country is just one testament to that, as are oyster festivals, shucking championships, slurp-offs, and countless other places where oyster fans congregate.

An oyster's striking character is evident from first glance at the rugged, cupped shell that blends in beautifully with its natural environment of rocky beaches and tide flats. Sometimes the shells even carry evidence of that environment, with small barnacles or tufts of seaweed clinging to them. And some are extravagantly fluted, almost (but not quite) too pretty to shuck.

Inside is the most wondrous of little virtual vacations, transporting you to the body of water where the oyster lived. Oysters are filter-feeders, drawing many gallons of water through their shells each day to collect nutrients. The characteristics of that water contribute to the flavor and texture of the oyster. This taste of place, or "meroir," if you will, is one of the most compelling aspects that draw oyster lovers. And it makes sitting down to slurp a few different types such a treat. There's no better way to appreciate their distinct character than to taste them side by side.

Once an oyster is cooked, nuances are less evident. Which brings up a dividing line for some oyster eaters: those who only eat them raw, others who only eat them cooked. Though there are plenty of people like me who happily consume them whichever way they're served. (Sure, I'll acknowledge, too, those who have not yet worked up the courage to try an oyster at all.)

The two oyster varieties most widely available in the United States are the native Eastern oyster found from Texas to Maine and points north, and the Pacific oyster, which was introduced in the early twentieth century from Japan, found from California (and points south) to Alaska. You'll rarely see them sold by the species name, however. Instead they'll usually have a name indicating the body of water they came from, or perhaps a branded name that still traces back to a particular region or grower. This is because of those aforementioned variances in character that come from the oyster's habitat. Those two species take on an incredible array of guises, and flavors, based on locale.

A few other oysters you may come across include the Kumamoto oyster, another transplant from Japan that is particularly popular as a slurping oyster—you may see it more in oyster bars than in seafood markets. Same for the West Coast's only native oyster, the tiny Olympia oyster, with bold flavor that is also prized for enjoying raw. The fifth species is another transplant, this from across the Atlantic instead: The European flat oyster was introduced to Maine in the 1950s, where it sometimes goes by Belon, a French river renowned for flat oysters. Over time a population began to sustain itself naturally in the state—available in quite small volumes, the European flat is a specialty oyster. It is sometimes available from a few farming operations on the West Coast as well.

Though there is some wild harvest of oysters, most of what we buy will have been farm-raised, which means a ready supply from most growing regions throughout the year. Aficionados will indulge a bit more over winter and into early spring, when colder waters mean oysters are at their crispest, most plump, and most flavorful.

You may see oysters referred to as "tumbled." There are a few ways that process is done, but basically it's a way growers manage the oyster's growth so that it develops a deeper cup and plumper meat—all the better to be appreciated at the oyster bar when slurped.

Shopping and Storing

Oysters in their shells must be alive up to the point that you cook or shuck them. It's most common to buy oysters in the shell by the piece rather than by weight.

Another option for oysters is pre-shucked in jars or tubs. They come in various sizes, both in terms of the container itself (8 ounces to 16 ounces or more) and the size of the oysters inside (see page 103). I love this option for cooked oyster recipes, perfect for pan-fried and baked preparations. But not for slurping raw; save that pleasure for freshly shucked oysters.

Oyster shells are less susceptible to breakage than are clam and mussel shells, and they tend to gape less as well. You should still confirm that the oysters you buy have unbroken shells that are firmly closed—or that shut tightly when tapped. One extra test I apply is to tap two oysters together: it should sound like knocking two rocks together, a dull, solid sound. If an oyster sounds hollow, it will have lost a lot of its liquor that keeps it in prime form; I skip these oysters.

Get the oysters home and in the refrigerator as soon as you're able. If it's a warm day or the trip home not quick, ask for a bag of ice at the seafood counter to keep your oysters chilled in transit, or plan ahead and take along a cooler with a couple of frozen gel packs. Once home, I transfer the oysters to a colander set inside a bowl to catch any drips. Cover the oysters with a damp, not sopping wet, towel to keep them moist. Don't cover the bowl any more than that to ensure they get the air they need to survive. It's important that the oysters not sit in water, so don't be tempted to add ice or water to the bowl. If you have a lot of oysters, or if they're quite large, it may be easier to store them in a broad deep pan, like a roasting pan.

Cleaning

How much cleaning your in-shell oysters will need can vary. Those with smoother shells may harbor little in the way of sand or grit, needing just a quick rinse under cold running water. Those with more fluted or otherwise elaborate shells may need a touch of scrubbing. If you plan to serve them in the shell, cleaning the shells ensures a tidier presentation and avoids grit getting inside the oyster. If you'll be using just the oyster meat, it still pays to briefly toss the oysters under cold running water.

Cooking

To some, oysters never, or rarely, require any cooking. Nor any other ingredients, honestly. For devotees, the liquor that surrounds it in the shell is all the adornment a slurped oyster needs. Otherwise, a squeeze of lemon, splash of mignonette, or dash of hot sauce are among the ways to accent the briny treat in raw form.

Cooked in the shell, oysters are perfect on the grill. It can be as simple as putting the whole cleaned oysters directly on the grill (cupped side down) and cooking until they pop open. I prefer grilling oysters shucked, though, because it's easier to monitor the progress and you can add a flavor accent, such as seasoned butter, that cooks with the oyster. Shucked oysters also bake beautifully.

Out of the shell, I think one of the perfect options is pan-fried oysters. Pick your coating—flour, cracker crumbs, cornmeal, and beyond—and cook until nicely browned. It's hard to go wrong. Shucked oysters shine too, in stews, in gratins, deep-fried, and poached.

SHUCKING OYSTERS

If you have a heavy-duty shucking glove, here's the time to use it. Otherwise a thick kitchen towel works great too. You're protecting your hand from not only any potential slip of the shucking knife, but also from the often-sharp edges of the oyster shell. Fold the towel lengthwise in thirds on the counter, producing a few layers of thickness. Set the oyster on the towel near one end, with its cupped side down and pointed hinge end facing your dominant hand. Fold the rest of the towel up and over the oyster, holding the oyster down toward the rounded end with your nondominant hand and leaving the hinge still exposed.

1. Firmly grasp a good oyster knife (page 8) and use the tip to wedge carefully between the oyster halves at the hinge. Sometimes this is easy, and sometimes it takes determination. Keep at it and you will find the hinge gives and the knife tip will slip between the shells. The trick is to have *just* the tip of the knife slip in, rather than barging in with the whole blade. The latter is not a catastrophe, but it often means the oyster meat will be a bit marred.

2. Once the blade tip has slipped in, twist the knife handle to pry apart the shells.

3. Run the blade of the knife flat against the top shell of the oyster, separating the adductor muscle. To give you an idea of where to direct your efforts, the muscle is in roughly the top-right quarter portion of the oyster relative to the hinge.

4. Lift off and discard the top shell and gently slide the knife blade under the oyster as well, to slice through the other end of the adductor muscle and fully separate the oyster.

5. If serving the oysters on the half shell, arrange them on ice. Otherwise, proceed as directed for the recipe.

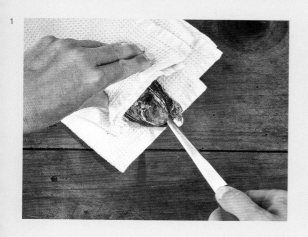

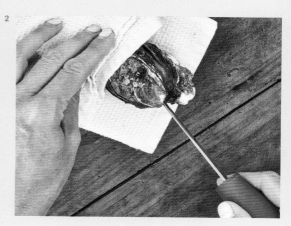

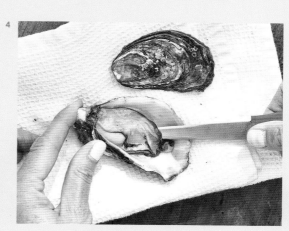

Half-Shell Oysters

with Cucumber Mignonette

How many servings do you get from a dozen half-shell oysters? It's something of a trick question. For some, one or two raw oysters is plenty in one sitting, for others a dozen might be just the warm-up. So consider your audience and plan accordingly. You should have enough cucumber to make a double batch of mignonette, doubling the other ingredients as well.

Makes 2 dozen oysters and a scant ½ cup mignonette

- 1 small English cucumber, peeled, or regular cucumber, peeled and seeded (about 12 ounces)
- 3 tablespoons Champagne or white wine vinegar
- 1 teaspoon minced shallot
- Freshly ground black pepper
- 24 small to medium live oysters, shells well rinsed

1   Coarsely grate about half of the cucumber and put it in a fine-mesh sieve set over a small bowl. Squeeze the cucumber in your hand to extract enough juice to measure 3 tablespoons. Mince enough of the remaining cucumber to measure 1 tablespoon. Save the remaining cucumber for another use, or just snack away.

2   In a small ramekin or other small serving dish, combine the cucumber juice, minced cucumber, vinegar, shallot, and a few grindings of black pepper and stir to mix. Refrigerate until ready to serve, up to 2 hours ahead.

3   Arrange crushed ice or rock salt on a rimmed serving tray (see sidebar). Shuck the oysters (see page 90) and nestle them into the ice, leaving room in the center for the mignonette, or simply serve the mignonette alongside. Have a small spoon in the mignonette so a drizzle can be added to each oyster just before slurping. →

SERVING HALF-SHELL OYSTERS

Perching oysters on ice for serving accomplishes two goals: keeping the oysters chilled and providing something for shells to nestle into so they don't tip and lose their liquor. Chunky ice cubes aren't much help; crushed ice is much more amenable to the task. Choose a tray or platter with a rim to contain the ice-melt, even if that's just a baking sheet. Guests will be more focused on the beautiful oysters than what they're served in.

In a pinch, rock salt can be used, accomplishing just the second benefit of the ice. Be sure you're shucking and serving these oysters right away so they are at their coldest.

Oysters Baked

with Horseradish Bread Crumbs

Freshly made and lightly toasted bread crumbs have a texture both light and crisp, ideal for this use. As a shortcut, panko crumbs are a decent substitute; they won't need the toasting step. For an extra punch of horseradish, grate a bit more over the oysters just before serving, if you're using fresh. Braised or steamed greens with lemon will round out these oysters as a main-course offering; they're also great as an appetizer. For an out-of-shell option, you could use jarred oysters (see page 103) and bake them in a shallow, buttered baking dish with the crumb mixture spread evenly on top; they'll need 15 to 18 minutes baking time.

Makes 2 main-course or 4 to 6 appetizer servings

- 1 cup fresh bread crumbs (see note) or panko crumbs
- 12 medium live oysters, shells well rinsed
- 3 tablespoons finely grated fresh horseradish, or 2 tablespoons prepared horseradish

- 3 tablespoons unsalted butter, melted
- ½ teaspoon kosher salt
- Freshly ground black pepper

1   Preheat the oven to 400 degrees F. Line a rimmed baking sheet with rock salt or cut a piece of aluminum foil twice as long as the baking sheet and crumple it to evenly cover the bottom of the baking sheet, which will help the oyster shells sit evenly.

2   Put the fresh bread crumbs in a small baking pan, like a cake pan or pie pan. Lightly toast them in the oven, 5 to 7 minutes, stirring two or three times. The crumbs need not brown evenly, just a bit of color is good. Set aside to cool. Leave the oven set at 400 degrees F. →

3   Shuck the oysters (see page 90). Pour off excess liquor so it won't make the crumb topping too soggy, and nestle the oysters into the rock salt or foil so that they sit evenly.

4   If using fresh horseradish, combine it with the bread crumbs in a small bowl and toss well with a fork to mix. Drizzle the butter over, add the salt and few grindings of black pepper, and toss well to mix. If using prepared horseradish, stir it together with the melted butter in a small bowl, then add the bread crumbs, salt, and pepper and toss well to mix.

5   Top the oysters with the bread crumbs, spreading to evenly cover each oyster. Bake until the oysters are plump, crumbs browned, and juices around the edges bubbling, 8 to 10 minutes. Use tongs to transfer the oysters to individual plates, perching them as evenly as you're able. Serve right away.

NOTE: One to two slices of regular white sandwich bread should be plenty for the 1 cup bread crumbs here; extra crumbs can be saved for another use. Tear each bread slice into 5 or 6 pieces and pulse them in a food processor to a relatively even texture of fine crumbs. (I don't bother removing the crusts; seems a waste unless you have another use for them.) The fresh crumbs can be used as is for some recipes, but in this case, they'll be toasted a bit for the best texture as an oyster topping.

Grilled Oysters Marinière

I'm mixing things up a bit with this combination of wine, shallot, butter, and herbs that is often used for steaming mussels. The flavors apply beautifully to grilled oysters as well. If you happen to have lemon thyme available, this is a great time to use it. It's easy enough to skip the wine if you prefer; they're delicious either way. Add crusty bread and coleslaw or another favorite salad to make this a meal for two. It's simple to double, if you'd like to grill a couple dozen oysters instead.

One small trick with grilling oysters is that the cupped shells (some more deeply cupped than others) take some care to perch evenly on the grill grate. It's a technique worth lots of practice, even after you get it down!

Makes 2 to 4 servings

- 4 tablespoons unsalted butter, at room temperature
- 2 tablespoons minced shallot
- 2 tablespoons minced fresh flat-leaf parsley
- ½ teaspoon minced fresh thyme (lemon or traditional)
- ¼ teaspoon kosher salt
- 12 medium to large live oysters, shells well rinsed
- 2 tablespoons dry white wine, divided (optional)

1 Combine the butter, shallot, parsley, thyme, and salt in a small bowl and stir well to thoroughly blend.

2 Preheat an outdoor grill for direct medium-high heat.

3 Shuck the oysters (see page 90). A little oyster liquor is fine, but pour off excess if there is quite a lot in some of the shells. Arrange the oysters on a tray perched as evenly as you can manage.

4 Spoon a generous teaspoon of the butter mixture onto each oyster and add about ½ teaspoon of wine to each shell. Use long-handled tongs to transfer the →

oysters to the preheated grill, perching the shells as evenly as you're able. Grill until the oysters are plump, their edges curled, and buttery juices bubbling, 6 to 9 minutes. Use the tongs to carefully transfer oysters to a platter or individual plates, preserving as much of the flavorful liquids in the shell as you can en route.

Cornmeal-Fried Oysters

with Pickled-Pepper Tartar Sauce

Pan-fried oysters rank as one of my all-time favorite preparations for the lovely bivalves. There are lots of options for the coating; here, I use cornmeal to add a bit of nutty-crunchy character. The tartar sauce uses pickled peppers in place of dill pickles, with flavor as potentially varied—and spicy—as the type of pepper you use. Pepperoncini are a great option, and I love using Mama Lil's peppers as well. A cucumber-tomato salad would complement the rich oysters well.

Makes 2 main-course or 4 to 6 appetizer servings

For the pickled-pepper tartar sauce

- ¾ cup mayonnaise
- 3 to 4 tablespoons finely chopped pickled peppers
- 2 tablespoons finely chopped fresh flat-leaf parsley or chives
- 2 tablespoons finely chopped green onion, white and light-green portions
- 1 tablespoon white wine vinegar or freshly squeezed lemon juice
- ¼ teaspoon kosher salt

- 1¼ cups fine cornmeal, plus more for sprinkling
- 1 teaspoon kosher salt
- ½ teaspoon freshly ground black pepper
- 24 medium freshly shucked (see page 90) or jarred oysters (see page 103)
- Vegetable or other neutral oil, for cooking

1   To make the tartar sauce, combine the mayonnaise, pickled peppers, parsley, green onion, vinegar, and salt in a small bowl and stir well to mix. Taste for seasoning, adding more pickled peppers or salt if needed, though keep in mind that flavors will develop a bit over time. Cover and refrigerate until ready to serve. (The sauce can be made a day ahead.)

2   Preheat the oven to 200 degrees F. Set an oblong wire rack on a rimmed baking sheet. Sprinkle a thin layer of cornmeal across the bottom of another rimmed baking sheet or tray. →

3   Combine the cornmeal, salt, and pepper in a medium bowl and stir with a fork to combine. Add a few of the oysters to the cornmeal and toss with the fork to evenly coat. Pat to remove excess cornmeal from the oysters and set them, not touching each other, on the baking sheet sprinkled with cornmeal. Continue coating the remaining oysters.

4   Heat about ¼ inch of oil in a large heavy skillet, such as cast iron, over medium-high heat.

5   When the oil is heated, carefully add 6 to 8 of the oysters without crowding them (cook fewer if needed) and cook until nicely browned, about 3 minutes; if the oysters are browning too quickly, reduce the heat to medium. Note that the oysters may spatter as they give off liquid while frying. Turn the oysters and brown on the second side, 2 to 3 minutes longer. Transfer the oysters to the baking sheet with the wire rack and keep warm in the oven while frying the remaining oysters. Add a bit more oil to the skillet and allow to reheat as needed between batches.

6   Arrange the fried oysters on individual plates, add a generous dollop of the tartar sauce alongside, and serve right away, passing extra tartar sauce separately.

JARRED OYSTERS

By jarred oysters, I mean those that are sold shucked and available in the seafood case in jars or tubs. Sizes vary, both for the container (8 ounces to 16 ounces or more) and for the oysters inside. I find extra-small to be consistently available and an ideal size for most recipes, really more of a medium-size oyster in general terms. This size is a good choice for use in these recipes.

There are also smaller "yearling" oysters and larger "small," sometimes "medium," size as well, the latter being actually quite large. East Coast and Gulf oysters can be sold by different grades, from smaller "standard" up to larger "count" oysters.

Note that the exact number of oysters you'll get from a jar is not certain. By very rough average, I've found a 10-ounce jar or tub of extra-small Pacific oysters may have about 10 oysters, sometimes 8 or fewer, sometimes 12. You can save any extra oysters for another preparation the next day; simply toss with seasoned cornmeal or flour to pan-fry. Or the Baked Oysters with Bacon and Eggs (page 104), using just 4 oysters, is a great option.

Baked Oysters
with Bacon and Eggs

Perfect for breakfast or brunch, this recipe can just as well swing into lunch or even dinnertime, with green salad and fried potatoes alongside. I find the bacon often prevents the egg from sticking to the ramekin, so you may be able to turn these out for serving if you'd like. Some oysters in your jar may be smaller than others, in which case you can double up a couple of smaller oysters. Extra oysters from the container will be great in Cornmeal-Fried Oysters (page 101).

The oysters are going to give off a bit of liquid as they cook, which can be easy to mistake for uncooked egg. Do your best to test for doneness in the cooked egg; the texture should be firm when pressed as well.

Makes 4 servings

- 6 slices bacon, not thick-cut
- 4 large eggs
- 2 tablespoons half-and-half or whole milk
- 2 tablespoons finely chopped chives or green onion tops

- Kosher salt and freshly ground black pepper
- 4 small freshly shucked (see page 90) or jarred oysters (see page 103), well drained
- Toast, for serving

1 Preheat the oven to 450 degrees F. Line a rimmed baking sheet with aluminum foil. Lightly butter 4 ramekins of about ½-cup volume.

2 Lay the bacon on the prepared baking sheet and bake until it has given off a good bit of its fat, 4 to 6 minutes. Turn the pieces over and continue baking until just lightly browned, but not crisp, about 5 minutes longer. Transfer the bacon to paper towels to drain. Reduce the oven temperature to 375 degrees F.

3 When the bacon is cool, line the inside edge of each ramekin with 1 piece of the bacon, upright against the sides, with the ends of the bacon overlapping if needed. Cut the remaining pieces of bacon in half crosswise and lay a piece

on the bottom of each ramekin, with the ends coming up the sides. Set the ramekins on a baking sheet.

4   Lightly beat the eggs in a medium bowl, then add the half-and-half and chives with a good pinch of salt and a few grindings of pepper.

5   Add 1 oyster to each ramekin, then pour in the egg mixture to reach just below the rim of the ramekins. Bake until the eggs puff up nicely and are cooked through (a knife inserted into the cooked egg, rather than the oyster, will come out clean), 15 to 20 minutes.

6   Transfer the ramekins to individual plates and serve right away, with toast alongside.

Oysters à la Falafel in Pita

The nutty-herbal-spiced character of falafel becomes a coating for fried oysters in this recipe. They're served on warm pita bread, with bright, crisp vegetables and a zippy tahini drizzle. The pita can be halved, filling each pouch, or served whole as a wrap. Or skip the pita, simply serving the oysters on a bed of the vegetables, drizzled with sauce. Add a cucumber-yogurt salad or roasted vegetables alongside to make for a more substantial meal.

Look for chickpea flour, also known as garbanzo bean flour, with other specialty flours or other Mediterranean ingredients.

Makes 4 servings

For the oysters
- 12 medium freshly shucked (see page 90) or jarred oysters (see page 103)
- 1 cup chickpea flour
- ¼ cup finely chopped fresh flat-leaf parsley
- ½ teaspoon ground cumin
- ½ teaspoon kosher salt
- ¼ teaspoon garlic powder
- Pinch dried red pepper flakes or freshly ground black pepper
- ⅔ cup water, plus more if needed

For the tahini sauce
- ¼ cup plain whole-milk or low-fat yogurt
- 3 tablespoons freshly squeezed lemon juice, plus more if needed
- 2 tablespoons tahini
- ¼ teaspoon kosher salt

- Vegetable oil or other neutral oil, for frying
- ½ cup finely shredded red cabbage
- ½ cup grated carrot
- ½ cup finely chopped cucumber
- 2 to 4 pita breads, warmed

1   Preheat the oven to 200 degrees F. Set an oblong wire rack on a rimmed baking sheet.

2   To prepare the oysters, first drain the oysters on paper towels, with another piece of paper towel pressed on top.

3   Use a fork to stir together the chickpea flour, parsley, cumin, salt, garlic powder, and pepper flakes in a medium bowl. Add the water in a slow stream, stirring constantly to form a smooth batter. This will be a rather thick batter, but if it's a bit too thick to easily coat the oysters, stir in another 1 to 2 tablespoons water.

4   To make the tahini sauce, stir together the yogurt, lemon juice, tahini, and salt in a small bowl until smooth. The sauce should be thin enough to drizzle, stir in extra lemon juice or a bit of water if needed.

5   Add enough oil to a large heavy skillet (cast iron is ideal) so it is about ¼ inch deep. Heat the oil over medium-high heat.

6   Drop a few oysters into the batter and turn them with the fork to evenly coat. Lift out one oyster at a time, allowing excess batter to drip off, and carefully add it to the skillet. Repeat with a few more oysters, careful to not crowd them in the skillet to ensure even cooking. Cook until nicely browned on one side, 3 to 4 minutes, reducing the heat a bit if the oysters are browning too quickly. Note that the oysters may spatter as they give off liquid while frying. Gently turn the oysters and cook until browned on the second side, 2 to 3 minutes longer. Transfer the fried oysters to the baking sheet and keep warm in the oven. Continue with the remaining oysters, adding a bit more oil to the skillet if needed.

7   To serve, distribute the red cabbage, carrot, and cucumber evenly among the pita breads (on top for a wrap, or in the pouch if halved) and top with the fried oysters. Drizzle some of the tahini sauce over and serve right away, passing extra sauce separately.

Smoked Oyster Dip

This simple dip can be made with other shellfish. Consider other smoked options—such as clams or mussels—or cooked shrimp, clams, or crabmeat, adding a bit more of these if you like since they're milder than the smoked options. The flavor will be best if made a couple of hours ahead, and the dip holds well for a couple of days in the refrigerator. If the smoked oysters you're using are packed in oil, drain them on paper towels before using.

Makes about 2 cups

- 8 ounces cream cheese, at room temperature
- ½ cup sour cream
- 3 to 4 ounces smoked oysters, finely chopped (see note)
- ¼ cup finely chopped green onion, white and green parts
- 1 teaspoon finely grated lemon zest
- 2 tablespoons freshly squeezed lemon juice
- ½ teaspoon Worcestershire sauce
- ½ teaspoon kosher salt
- A few dashes Tabasco sauce or other hot sauce
- Thick-cut potato chips, pita chips, or crackers, for serving

1. In a medium bowl, combine the cream cheese and sour cream and stir with a rubber spatula until well blended and smooth. If the cream cheese still shows some lumps, let it sit for a bit longer to fully soften.

2. Add the smoked oysters, green onion, lemon zest, lemon juice, Worcestershire sauce, salt, and Tabasco. Stir gently to mix well, then taste for seasoning, adding more salt to taste. Transfer the dip to a serving bowl, cover, and refrigerate until ready to serve, preferably for at least 2 hours.

3. Serve the dip with potato chips alongside.

NOTE: You may see smoked oysters with various flavors; I think the classic smoked oyster works best here. Package and can sizes vary, ideally you'll have about 1 cup chopped to use, though a 3-ounce can may leave you shy. I found it was still tasty at that amount; it's up to you if you want to open a second can.

Shrimp

I won't be surprised if this is the section of the book that most folks turn to first. Of all the shellfish in the sea, shrimp are without a doubt the most loved: easy to cook, mild in flavor, and extremely versatile, both in terms of potential cooking methods and flavor combinations. It's the number one seafood consumed in the United States, and has been in that spot for some time.

Shrimp are so ubiquitous that it can be easy to take their supply for granted, and think that a shrimp is a shrimp is a shrimp. But there are distinctions to look for, with regard to species and provenance in particular. Add questions of sustainability to the mix—which are particularly varied with this globally produced shellfish—and the consumer has a number of things to consider with shrimp.

The most common species of larger shrimp harvested in the United States are white, brown, and pink shrimp, the first two in the greatest volumes. These shrimp are caught primarily in the Gulf of Mexico. The range for commercial harvest of the shrimp wraps around Florida and continues up the Atlantic coast as far as North Carolina.

Tiny little pink shrimp found on the West Coast are a different species from the Gulf pink shrimp. These shrimp are sold cooked and peeled, and can go by a number of names including bay shrimp or salad shrimp. Found from British Columbia to Southern California, the bulk of harvest is off the coast of Oregon. Thus another of their possible names, Oregon pink shrimp. These are sometimes referred to as cold-water shrimp, in contrast to those from the warmer waters of the Gulf.

Regional and seasonal shrimp varieties you may come across include spot prawns from Alaska and the Pacific Northwest and royal red shrimp from the Gulf. I've been fortunate to enjoy the former more than a few times, and have yet to get a taste of the latter. It's on my list.

White, brown, and pink shrimp are harvested year-round, though harvest is at lower volumes through the first few months of the year, and are available fresh and frozen. Oregon's pink shrimp season runs April through October, when fresh shrimp can be found, with frozen product readily available year-round as well.

Shopping and Storing

Shrimp are found in an array of forms. Head-on shrimp are something of a specialty item; most will be just the tail meat. These shrimp might be sold as is with the full shell intact. Or there may be a slit the length of the shell, which allows the vein to be removed in advance and makes the shell easier for you to peel away. Or the shrimp may have been peeled and deveined, with or without the last bit of fan-tipped tail still intact.

So should you buy shrimp with the shell on or off? For a simple shrimp boil or when cooking shrimp for another use, shell-on offers maximum flavor and helps keep the shrimp moist. Even if I'll be cooking the shrimp peeled, I prefer buying shrimp shell-on so I've got shells for making either a quick shrimp stock (see page 184) or batch of Shellfish Stock (page 183).

Sometimes shrimp are just sold as "shrimp," with little detail beyond perhaps confirming that it is raw or cooked, peeled or not. A general size, such a small or jumbo, may be noted, if not the more specific size grades used by the industry, such as "26/30" or "U-15". These sizes indicate how many shrimp—more or less—it takes to make a pound, with the U meaning "under." So for these examples, 26 to 30 shrimp per pound, and 15 or fewer shrimp per pound. The smaller the number, the bigger the shrimp.

As long as there's no excess liquid in the packaging for the shrimp you brought home, it should be fine to store them as is in the refrigerator for a day or two. Though the sooner you cook them, the better they'll be. Frozen shrimp should go into the freezer as quickly as you can manage to avoid any premature thaw, unless you intend to thaw right away to use soon. Otherwise, plan ahead to thaw overnight in the refrigerator. Don't refreeze thawed shrimp; it won't do the quality any favors.

Cleaning

The "vein" referenced in the "peel and devein" step of preparing shrimp is the digestive tract that runs along the back of the shrimp. It's more visible in some shrimp than others, often dark gray or black. It's easy enough to remove if it hasn't been already. Use the tip of a small knife to make a shallow slit along the back of the peeled shrimp, open the slit, and pull out the vein to discard. Otherwise, shrimp need little in the way of cleaning: I just given them a quick toss in a colander under cold running water and dry thoroughly before cooking.

Cooking

Shrimp are one of the easiest shellfish for home cooks to rely on. For the recipes I've included here, you'll see them grilled, deep-fried (how could I not!), marinated, sautéed, as a decadent sandwich, and baked a couple of ways. This is just a small drop in the bucket of potential options for enjoying this popular shellfish.

When I call for "peeled" shrimp in recipes, it's usually up to you if you want to leave the last bit of tail intact. Where it definitely needs to be removed, I'll point that out. When using peeled shrimp, it's worth taking the time to confirm there are no lingering bits of shell before cooking.

SHRIMP TAILS

I'm not against the pleasing aesthetics of leaving tails on the otherwise-peeled shrimp for recipes that serve the shrimp whole—they add some visual appeal and can serve as a handy little holder for eating the shrimp with your fingers. When a dish requires silverware, it becomes a bit messy navigating the tails, so I tend to remove them before cooking in those cases.

Sautéed Shrimp

with Garlic and Crisp Rosemary

One of the simplest and most delicious preparations for shrimp is a quick sauté in a hot skillet, with many possibilities for embellishment. I opt here for the aromatic combination of garlic and rosemary, the latter cooked until crisp.

Makes 4 to 6 servings

- ¼ cup unsalted butter
- 2 tablespoons fresh whole rosemary leaves
- 3 cloves garlic, thinly sliced
- 1½ pounds large shrimp, peeled, deveined, and rinsed

- Kosher salt and freshly ground black pepper
- ½ cup dry white wine, shrimp stock (see page 184), or Shellfish Stock (page 183)
- 2 tablespoons freshly squeezed lemon juice

1   Melt the butter in a large skillet over medium heat. Add the rosemary and cook, stirring occasionally with a fork, until the rosemary is lightly crisped, aromatic, and just beginning to lightly brown, about 2 minutes (too brown and it becomes a tad bitter). Note that the butter will brown as it cooks, which is a good thing, adding a bit of nutty flavor as well. Take the skillet from the heat and use the fork to lift out the rosemary onto a small plate, allowing excess butter to drip back into the skillet. Set the rosemary aside to cool.

2   Return the skillet to medium heat and add the garlic. Cook, stirring often with a wooden spoon, until aromatic, 30 to 60 seconds. Add the shrimp with a good pinch of salt and a few grindings of black pepper and cook, stirring occasionally, until the shrimp are evenly opaque on the surface, 2 to 3 minutes. Add the wine and simmer over medium-high heat until the sauce is reduced by about half and the shrimp are just cooked through (opaque through the thickest part), 3 to 4 minutes longer. Take the skillet from the heat, stir in the lemon juice, taste the sauce for seasoning, and add more salt or pepper to taste.

3   Spoon the shrimp and sauce onto individual plates, sprinkle the crisp rosemary over, and serve right away.

Grilled Shrimp

on Lentil-Arugula Salad

Since shrimp don't need much time on the grill, consider planning to cook
something else on the grill while it's hot. Maybe skewers of mushrooms
and zucchini to serve alongside, and pieces of rustic bread brushed
with olive oil to grill-toast. I always have French green lentils on hand,
occasionally black "beluga" or "caviar" lentils, so named for their small,
nearly round shape reminiscent of caviar. Both hold their shape well when
cooked, great for countless uses. Regular green or brown lentils are good
too; they just may get a tad softer. The vinaigrette gets double duty here:
part used to marinate the shrimp, the rest for dressing the salad.

Makes 4 servings

For the vinaigrette
- 3 tablespoons white wine vinegar
- 2 teaspoons Dijon mustard
- ¼ teaspoon kosher salt
- Freshly ground black pepper
- ⅓ cup extra-virgin olive oil or mild
  olive oil

- 1 pound medium to large shrimp,
  peeled, deveined, and rinsed

- 1 teaspoon kosher salt
- 1 bay leaf, preferably fresh
- 1 clove garlic
- ¾ cup green or black lentils, rinsed
- 4 cups loosely packed arugula
  (about 3 ounces)
- ¼ cup thinly sliced green onion
  (white and green parts), or 2
  tablespoons chopped fresh chives

1   If using bamboo skewers, soak four 8- to 10-inch bamboo skewers in cold water
    for at least 20 minutes to limit charring on the grill.

2   To make the vinaigrette, whisk together the vinegar, mustard, salt, and a couple of
    grindings of pepper in a large bowl until the salt is dissolved, then whisk in the oil.

3   Put the shrimp in a medium bowl. Rewhisk the vinaigrette to blend, and drizzle
    about half of it over the shrimp. Toss the shrimp to evenly coat, cover the bowl,
    and refrigerate while cooking the lentils. →

4   Half-fill a medium saucepan with water and add the salt, bay leaf, and whole garlic clove. Bring the water to a boil over high heat. Add the lentils, reduce the heat to medium-low, and simmer uncovered until the lentils are just tender, 18 to 22 minutes. Drain the lentils, discarding the bay leaf but reserving the garlic with the lentils. Set aside to cool (I set the strainer over the pan the lentils cooked in to allow excess water to drain away as they sit).

5   Preheat an outdoor grill for direct medium-high heat.

6   Lift the garlic clove from the cooked lentils, flicking any clinging lentils back with the others (if the garlic has fallen apart and mixed with the lentils, leave it as is). Add the soft garlic to the remaining vinaigrette and mash with a fork to blend. Add the cooled lentils and stir to evenly coat. Add the arugula and green onion and toss to mix, then arrange the salad on individual plates, slightly mounded in the center.

7   Thread the marinated shrimp onto 4 skewers, catching the tail and broad end of each to form a C as they go on the skewers. Grill the shrimp until just opaque through the thickest part, 2 to 3 minutes per side.

8   Lean a skewer of shrimp against each salad, or remove the shrimp from the skewers to perch on the salad, and serve right away.

Harissa-Roasted Shrimp, Carrots, and Radishes

Shrimp get colorful and flavorful accents from carrots and radishes, which are sometimes available in hues beyond their classic orange and red. If you happen to find extra-small carrots—finger-slender and about 4 inches long or less—they can be roasted whole. The harissa I use is the paste type, a staple in my fridge. It comes in varying styles, including varying degrees of heat, so use more or less to suit your taste. You can find it in powdered form as well. Either will work, though an extra drizzle of olive oil may be needed if using powder. This could be served with, or over, couscous or orzo.

Makes 4 servings

- 12 ounces small to medium carrots, trimmed
- 2 bunches radishes, trimmed
- ¼ cup mild olive oil, plus more if needed
- 1 to 2 tablespoons harissa

- ¾ teaspoon ground cumin
- ½ teaspoon ground coriander
- ½ teaspoon kosher salt
- 1½ pounds medium to large shrimp, peeled, deveined, and rinsed

1   Preheat the oven to 450 degrees F.

2   Cut larger carrots into 3– to 4–inch lengths, and then cut in half or quarters so they're not much more than ½ inch wide; extra-small carrots can be used as is. Small radishes can be cooked as is; medium or large radishes should be halved or quartered.

3   Combine the oil, harissa, cumin, coriander, and salt in a large bowl and use a rubber spatula to evenly mix the seasonings. Add the shrimp, carrots, and radishes and toss to evenly coat. If using dried harissa and the coating is a bit sparse, add another 1 or 2 tablespoons oil and toss again. →

4   Transfer the shrimp and vegetables to a rimmed baking sheet (see sidebar), spreading them out in an even layer with the shrimp toward the center and the vegetables around the edge. Use the spatula to get all the flavorful oil from the bowl onto the shrimp and vegetables. Roast until the carrots and radishes are just tender and the shrimp are opaque through the thickest part, 10 to 12 minutes.

5   Transfer the shrimp and vegetables to individual plates and serve right away.

SHEET PAN COOKING

The beauty of sheet pan cooking is the convenience of tossing things on the pan to roast together. The only trick is managing the components so they're done at the same time. In this case, carrots a bit too big may be crunchy when the shrimp are done, or the shrimp dry and tough if cooked longer to accommodate the carrots. Bigger shrimp give you more leeway; if you're using smaller shrimp or just want a bit of insurance, you can roast the vegetables for 5 minutes or so first, then add the shrimp at the center of the pan, in which case they'll cook a minute or two more quickly because the pan's preheated. In the long run, a slightly crunchy carrot or radish is better than an overcooked shrimp.

Fried Shrimp, Lemon, and Herbs

Given how big a fan base both shrimp and fried foods have, it's little wonder that fried shrimp are so popular. Here they are accompanied by thinly sliced lemon and tufts of fresh herbs—both of which also are lightly battered and quickly fried. I love these shrimp as is, but if you want a sauce alongside, consider the Pickled-Pepper Tartar Sauce (page 101). Shrimp with the tail on or off—it's up to you. If you have a deep fryer, of course here's the time to use it, following the manufacturer's instructions. A green salad or coleslaw will be perfect alongside.

Makes 4 servings

- 1 small lemon
- 1¼ pounds medium shrimp, peeled, deveined, and rinsed
- Vegetable oil, for frying
- ¾ cup all-purpose flour
- ½ cup cornstarch
- 1 teaspoon kosher salt
- 1 cup cold water, plus more if needed
- 2 handfuls (about 2 cups loosely packed) large flat fresh herb leaves, such as basil, shiso, flat-leaf parsley, and/or sage, rinsed and well dried

1   Preheat the oven to 200 degrees F. Set an oblong wire rack on a rimmed baking sheet.

2   Trim the ends from the lemon and cut it into slices about ⅛ inch thick, removing any seeds you encounter along the way. Dry the shrimp well on paper towels.

3   Heat about 2 inches of oil in a medium heavy pot (the oil should come no more than halfway up the sides of the pot) over medium heat to 375 degrees F.

4   While the oil heats, make the batter. Use a fork to stir together the flour, cornstarch, and salt in a medium bowl. Add the water gradually, blending to make a smooth batter. It should be thin enough to delicately coat the shrimp. If it's a bit too thick, stir in another 1 to 2 tablespoons water. →

5   Drop 5 or 6 shrimp into the batter and stir to coat. Lift them out one by one with the fork or tongs, allowing excess batter to drip off, then gently add them to the hot oil. Fry the shrimp until lightly browned, 3 to 4 minutes. Scoop them out with a slotted spoon, transfer to the prepared baking sheet, and keep warm in the oven. Continue to coat and fry the shrimp in batches, allowing the oil to reheat between batches as needed.

6   Add about a quarter of the herbs to the batter, coating well with the batter. Lift the leaves out one by one, allowing excess batter to drip off, and gently add to the oil. Fry each batch until crisp, 1 to 2 minutes. Add the fried herbs to the baking sheet with the shrimp. Cook the lemon slices in the same way, in two batches. Arrange the shrimp, lemon, and herbs on individual plates and serve right away.

Marinated Shrimp
with Sweet Onions

I've rejiggered one of my mom's favorite recipes from a 1950s *Better Homes & Gardens* cookbook (see sidebar) for this preparation that's perfect as the first course for a dinner party, cocktail party, or buffet dinner spread. Since the shrimp cook so quickly, I simmer the spices a bit to impart more flavor before adding the shrimp. The shrimp need to marinate for at least 8 hours, and up to 24 hours, so plan accordingly. This is a great do-ahead recipe.

Makes 8 to 10 servings

- 3 tablespoons pickling spice
- ½ cup moderately packed celery leaves
- 1 tablespoon plus 1 teaspoon kosher salt, divided
- 2 pounds medium to large shrimp, preferably shell-on, rinsed
- 1 small sweet onion (about 12 ounces), cut into ¼-inch rounds and separated into rings

- 6 bay leaves, preferably fresh
- ⅔ cup white wine vinegar
- ½ cup mild olive oil
- 2 tablespoons capers and their juice
- 2 teaspoons celery seed
- Tabasco or other hot sauce
- Watercress, frisée, and/or arugula, for serving

1   Cut a double layer of cheesecloth about 6 inches square. Put the pickling spice in the center, draw up the edges, and secure the packet with a piece of kitchen string. Put the spice packet, celery leaves, and 1 tablespoon of the salt in a medium pot half filled with water. Bring the water to a boil over medium-high heat and simmer for 10 minutes, pressing the spice packet down into the water now and then if it's floating at the surface. Carefully add the shrimp and simmer until opaque through the thickest part (lift one out with a slotted spoon and cut into it to check), 6 to 8 minutes. If the water boils at any point, reduce the heat a bit. Drain the shrimp, discarding the spice packet and celery leaves. When cool enough to handle, peel and devein the shrimp, unless they already have been. →

2   Put the shrimp, onion, and bay leaves in a 9-by-13-inch baking dish or similar deep dish, or in a large resealable plastic bag or other container. Stir together the vinegar, oil, capers and juice, celery seed, remaining 1 teaspoon of salt, and a few dashes of Tabasco (or to taste). Pour this evenly over the shrimp, cover or close the container, and refrigerate for at least 8 hours, and up to 24 hours, before serving. Gently stir or toss things around a few times to ensure even seasoning while they marinate.

3   To serve, arrange the greens on a serving platter or individual plates. Spoon the shrimp and onion onto the greens with just enough marinade to lightly coat; use a slotted spoon to retrieve any capers from the remaining marinade to scatter over.

NOSTALGIA AND SHRIMP

"Shell and devein and carry on," my mom wrote many years ago on the inside of a 1960s booklet with shellfish recipes produced by the Washington Department of Fisheries. It was part of her instructions related not to a recipe in that booklet but to one she said was a "favorite shrimp hors d'oeuvre which I've made dozens of times." She credited it to *Better Homes & Gardens New Cookbook*, her 1953 copy of which I have. Turning to that page, I see she wrote "The Greatest" in broad felt pen alongside the recipe, with a penciled note about having added mushrooms on occasion. My sister recalls this being a frequent element on a buffet spread, served in a shallow bowl with cocktail sauce alongside for those who might wish to dip.

Shrimp-Stuffed Eggplant

with Sesame

Chinese and Japanese eggplants are long and slender, smaller than the more common globe eggplant. Try to pick four that are of about the same size (length and width), for even cooking and portion sizes. Those that are straight or just slightly curved will be easiest to work with. Don't be tempted to chop the shrimp in a food processor; you want distinct small pieces rather than a near purée. This is delicious with sautéed bok choy or broccoli alongside, and steamed rice if you wish.

Makes 2 to 4 servings

- 4 Chinese or Japanese eggplants (about 8 ounces each)
- 2 tablespoons mild olive oil, plus more for drizzling
- ½ cup finely chopped shallot or onion
- 1 teaspoon minced or pressed garlic
- 12 ounces shrimp, peeled (tails too), deveined, rinsed, and chopped
- 4 tablespoons finely chopped fresh cilantro, divided
- 1 tablespoon finely chopped fresh mint
- 2 teaspoons toasted sesame oil
- ½ teaspoon kosher salt
- 1 tablespoon lightly toasted sesame seeds

1 Preheat the oven to 400 degrees F. Line a rimmed baking sheet with aluminum foil.

2 Trim the stem ends from the eggplants so what remains is more or less 7 inches long. Cut the top quarter or so of the eggplant off, "top" being relative: however the eggplant sits most naturally on the counter, determine the top from that position. Eggplant pieces that have been cut away can be saved for another use.

3 Use the tip of a small knife to score the flesh about ¼ inch in from the skin and about 1 inch deep, then use a spoon to scoop out this flesh, making a cavity for the shrimp mixture. Finely chop the scooped-out eggplant flesh.

4   Drizzle oil on the foil and set the eggplant shells cut side down on the baking sheet. Bake until the sides are tender (the tip of a sharp knife should meet little resistance), 10 to 15 minutes. Take the baking sheet from the oven and let cool while preparing the filling. Keep the oven set at 400 degrees F.

5   Heat the oil in a medium skillet over medium heat. Add the shallot, garlic, and chopped eggplant and cook, stirring often, until they are tender and turning golden, about 5 minutes. Transfer the mixture to a medium bowl and let cool. Stirring occasionally will help it cool a bit more quickly.

6   Add the chopped shrimp to the cooled shallot mixture along with 3 tablespoons of the cilantro, the mint, sesame oil, and salt and stir well to evenly blend. When the eggplants are cool enough to handle, turn them over and spoon the shrimp mixture into the cavities, pressing it in gently and mounding slightly. Sprinkle the sesame seeds over. Return the eggplants to the baking sheet and bake until the shrimp is cooked through (fully opaque when you peek into the center of the filling), about 20 minutes.

7   Transfer the eggplants to individual plates, scatter the remaining 1 tablespoon of cilantro over, and serve right away.

Shrimp Salad
with Garlic Bread

It's tempting to say, for the first step of this recipe, "Get yourself to Charleston, South Carolina, and buy some shrimp at Shem Creek." That was the starting point when I first made this shrimp salad, using cooked shrimp and garlic bread left over from a shrimp boil while on vacation there with friends. If you have shellfish or shrimp stock in the freezer, add extra flavor by cooking the shrimp in that instead of water. The cooking liquids are then reduced to create a flavorful addition to the shrimp salad. The shrimp can be cooked and the reduction made the day ahead, both covered and refrigerated.

For a shortcut, start with cooked shrimp, even little bay shrimp, and skip the simmering and reduction steps. You'll still have a very good shrimp salad. A broader, softer style of French bread, rather than a classic baguette, is best for the garlic bread.

Makes 4 servings

- 1¼ pounds small to medium shrimp in their shells, rinsed
- 2½ cups shrimp stock (see page 184), Shellfish Stock (page 183), or water
- ⅓ cup mayonnaise, plus more if needed
- ¼ cup finely chopped sweet onion
- 2 tablespoons minced fresh chives
- ¼ teaspoon kosher salt
- Freshly ground black pepper

For the garlic bread
- 6-inch piece French bread
- ¼ cup unsalted butter, at room temperature
- 1 tablespoon minced fresh chives
- 2 cloves garlic, minced or pressed
- ¼ teaspoon kosher salt

1   Put the shrimp in a medium saucepan and add enough stock to just cover the shrimp completely (if you don't have enough stock, add water as needed). Bring the stock to a low boil over medium-high heat, then reduce the heat to medium and simmer, stirring a couple of times to ensure even cooking, until the shrimp are opaque through the thickest part (lift one out with a slotted spoon and cut into it to check), about 4 to 7 minutes. Drain the shrimp, reserving the cooking liquids. Wash out the pan to use again.

2   When the shrimp are cool enough to handle, peel them (tails included) and set the meat aside. Put the shells in the medium saucepan and add 2 cups of the reserved cooking liquids, which should cover the shells about halfway. Bring just to a boil over medium-high heat, then reduce the heat to medium and simmer until quite aromatic and the liquids have reduced by about half, 10 to 15 minutes, stirring occasionally. Take the pan from the heat and strain the liquid, discard the shells, and return the liquid to the pan. Set the pan over medium heat and simmer until the liquids reduce to a volume of about 3 tablespoons, 15 to 20 minutes. The final stage of reduction can go quickly, so keep a close eye on things and reduce the heat if needed toward the end to avoid burning. Scrape the reduction into a small bowl and let cool completely.

3   Devein the shrimp if needed, then coarsely chop the meat and put it in a medium bowl. Add the cooled shrimp reduction, mayonnaise, onion, chives, salt, and a couple grindings of black pepper and stir well to mix. Cover and refrigerate until ready to serve.

4   Preheat the oven to 450 degrees F.

5   To make the garlic bread, halve the bread horizontally, then cut each half into 2 pieces. Use a small rubber spatula to stir together the butter, chives, garlic, and salt in a small bowl until smooth and well blended, then spread it evenly on the bread. Set the bread on a rimmed baking sheet and bake until aromatic and just lightly browned at the edges, 5 to 7 minutes.

6   Spoon the shrimp salad onto individual plates, with the garlic bread alongside. Or spoon the shrimp directly onto the garlic bread and serve as a decadent open-faced sandwich.

Lobster

Other shellfish have their moments to shine in fancy presentations, but lobster seems most naturally suited to a sense of elegance. Consider its reputation as an entrée of choice for celebratory occasions and romantic dinners. Though for those who live near the home waters of those lobster, they are equally—if even more passionately—associated with casual summertime meals outdoors with ice-cold beverages. Perhaps that makes lobster a bit of a chameleon, able to admirably adapt to its environment, with guests in shorts and flip-flops for a shoreside feast or dressed to the nines for a fancy dinner with Champagne. And lobster are suited to countless options in between.

The species we see most often is the cold-water American lobster, with a long narrow carapace, fan-tipped tail, antennae, and big claws that make its eight other legs look particularly spindly. One claw is a bit bigger, the "crusher" claw; the more slender one called the "pincher." These lobster have a range of mottled deep purple-green-blue-russet color tones when alive, turning a vivid orange-red when cooked. American lobster are found from North Carolina as far north as Newfoundland; the bulk of the US harvest is from the waters off Maine.

Other lobster species are found in warmer waters to the south, on both sides of the country. Spiny lobster are distinct from American lobster, having large tails and no claws, just oversized antennae. Florida, and points south, is prime harvest area for Caribbean spiny lobster, while on the West Coast, the California spiny lobster is caught primarily in, unsurprisingly, California waters.

These lobster are all wild harvest. American lobster are harvested year-round, peak season being July into November, when a greater supply generally results in lower prices. Other times of year, prices are more variable. The warm-water lobster are harvested most of fall and winter. Frozen offerings of lobster, particularly in tail form, can be found year-round.

Shopping and Storing

It's important that whole uncooked lobster be alive up until they're cooked. When buying live lobster, choose from among the livelier of the bunch. The range in size for American lobster is roughly 1¼ pounds up to 4 pounds, though 3 pounds and up are less common.

Raw American lobster tails are a quite convenient and widely available option year-round, in sizes from about 4 ounces up to 8 ounces or more. Spiny lobster tails are also versatile (seldom found in whole live form), though I see them less frequently in stores.

Cooked lobster meat may be available either in bulk in the seafood case, or prepackaged in containers. Also, you may see tails, meat, or other forms of lobster in the freezer section as well.

Live lobster manage rather well out of water in the right conditions, though you should plan to cook the lobster the same day you buy them. Store lobster in a container large enough to hold them comfortably, such as an oblong baking dish or large broad bowl. Top the lobster with a damp, not sopping wet, kitchen towel to keep it moist. Don't enclose the dish any more than that; the lobster need air to survive. Don't be tempted to store live lobster in water or with ice, as fresh water kills them.

Lobster tails and meat should be well wrapped and stored in the refrigerator until needed. If purchased in a frozen state, get them into your freezer as soon as possible after getting home to avoid any premature thawing. Plan ahead to thaw slowly in the refrigerator before using.

Cleaning

Whole lobster and lobster tails in the shell should require little cleaning before cooking, perhaps just a quick rinse under cold running water.

Cooking

When cooking live lobster, the change in shell color to vivid orange-red isn't the sole indicator for doneness; the meat may still be a bit undercooked at that point. To verify doneness after the suggested cooking time, lift the lobster from the pot and carefully (with pot holders) twist open where the tail meets the carapace and check the meat, which should be opaque white, no longer translucent.

I prefer steaming over boiling for a few reasons, which I discuss more on page 6. It means cooking for a couple of minutes longer, but it's a minor time adjustment for what I find to be a much easier process. These whole lobster are perfect to enjoy as is—with melted butter or a light sauce. They can be grilled or roasted as well.

Lobster tails can be grilled, roasted, or steamed, whether to serve as is, or to use the cooked meat in another dish. Cooked lobster meat, like cooked crabmeat, is quite versatile. Recipes using it here include a light stew, a sandwich, and a flavorful salad. Those handsome lobster have quite sharp points on their shells, so take care when handling them to avoid puncturing yourself.

PORTIONING COOKED LOBSTER

These steps can be followed if you are picking the meat from a cooked lobster for another use. If preparing the lobster to be served right away, how much advance prep you do depends on the setting: for a casual meal, diners can do this work themselves. Otherwise you can go through some or all of the process before serving so that eating is a bit less messy at the table.

1. Holding the lobster body in one hand and tail in the other, twist gently to separate the two.

2. Remove the front clawed legs from the body by bending them back where they meet the body. Separate the front legs into two sections, Use crab crackers or a small mallet to lightly crack the shell of the smaller knuckle joints, removing those nuggets.

3. For each claw, bend backward and remove the movable part from the claw, which should come out with a thin membrane attached.

4. Use crab crackers or a small mallet to lightly crack the claw shell, pulling the shell apart to remove the large piece of meat.

5. For the tail, use kitchen shears to cut through the membrane on the bottom, and pull the sides apart to remove the tail meat in one piece.

6. Use the tip of a small knife to make a slit in the top of the tail, then lift out and discard the vein.

NOTE: If you will use the body for Shellfish Stock (page 183) or wish to pick extra bits of meat from the body, lift away the top shell (carapace), then remove and discard the viscera, including the greenish tomalley. Rinse well under cold water. There is a bit of meat in the small walking legs as well, which you can pick if you like.

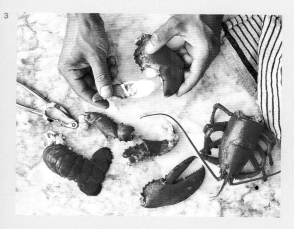

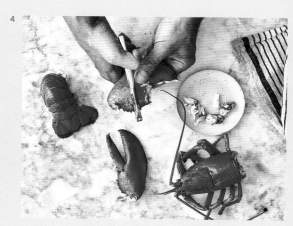

Grilled Lobster Tails and Summer Squash

with Gremolata Butter

Such a treat to pull from the grill, these lobster tails get slathered with a butter that's blended with the gremolata trio of parsley, garlic, and lemon zest. Standard zucchini and yellow squash can be found year-round, while summertime offerings may include small zucchini, pattypan squash, and other varieties—mix and match as inspired by what's available. While the grill's hot, consider cooking other things as well—thick slices of sweet onion, ears of corn—whether to serve alongside or to have on hand for other uses.

Makes 4 servings

For the gremolata butter
- 1 large lemon
- 6 tablespoons unsalted butter, at room temperature
- 2 tablespoons finely chopped fresh flat-leaf parsley
- ¼ teaspoon minced or pressed garlic
- ¼ teaspoon kosher salt

- 1 pound summer squash (zucchini, yellow squash, and/or pattypan squash)
- 2 tablespoons mild olive oil, divided, plus more if needed
- Kosher salt
- 4 lobster tails, 5 to 8 ounces each

1   For the gremolata butter, finely grate enough zest from the lemon to measure 1 teaspoon. Stir together the butter, parsley, lemon zest, garlic, and salt in a small bowl until smooth and well blended. Cut the lemon into 4 wedges; set the butter and lemon aside. →

2   Preheat an outdoor grill for direct medium-high heat. If using bamboo skewers, soak four 8- to 10-inch skewers in cold water for at least 20 minutes to limit charring on the grill.

3   Trim the stem ends from the squash. Cut zucchini or yellow squash across into 1-inch pieces. Larger pattypan can be cut into halves or quarters; small pattypan or other mini squash can be grilled whole (no skewer needed). Put the squash in a large bowl, drizzle 1 tablespoon of the oil over, and season with a good pinch of salt. Toss well to evenly coat. Thread the squash pieces onto the skewers, leaving a bit of space between them to help with even cooking; I find skewering from edge to edge, rather than through the center, ensures easier handling on the grill.

4   Set one of the lobster tails shell side up on the cutting board, its tail pointed away from you. Use the tip of a chef's knife to pierce the tail where it tapers to the narrow point just before the fanned end. Take care to avoid your fingers while lowering the blade down the length of the tail to cut it about three-quarters of the way through the meat. Bend the two shell halves apart a bit to expose more of the meat, avoiding those sharp bits on the shell. Remove and discard any visible vein running the length of the meat. Repeat with the remaining tails.

5   Brush the lobster meat and shell with the remaining tablespoon oil. Season the meat lightly with salt.

6   Grill the squash skewers until tender and nicely browned, 6 to 10 minutes, using long-handled tongs to turn them every couple of minutes to avoid excessive char. Transfer the skewers to a serving platter and cover with aluminum foil to keep warm. (Or if there is room on your grill, move the skewers to the edge, away from direct heat, to stay warm while grilling the lobster.)

7   Add the lobster tails to the grill, meat side down to begin with. Cook until the meat is just lightly browned, about 3 minutes. Use the tongs to turn the tails and continue cooking until the flesh is opaque through the thickest part, 3 to 6 minutes longer, depending on the size of the tails.

8   Transfer the lobster tails to individual plates and spread some of the gremolata butter on the meat. Add the grilled squash alongside (removed from the skewers if you like) and the lemon wedges, and serve right away. Pass extra gremolata butter separately for folks to dab on their squash and lobster.

Steamed Lobster

with Orange-Fennel Sauce

Steamed lobster with simple melted butter is perfectly sublime; this recipe just embellishes things. The flavors of orange and fennel, with a touch of vinegar, meld beautifully in this silky butter sauce for dipping. Look for a fennel bulb that has tender green fronds to use as a pretty and flavorful addition to the sauce. Extra fennel bulb can be thinly sliced to use in a green salad to serve alongside the lobster. Instead of using live lobster, you could use lobster tails instead, following the instructions on page 153 for cooking.

Makes 2 servings

- 2 live lobster, about 1½ pounds each
- 2 tablespoons kosher salt

  ───────────

  For the orange-fennel sauce
- ¾ cup freshly squeezed orange juice (from about 2 medium oranges)
- ¼ cup finely chopped fennel bulb

- 2 tablespoons minced shallot
- 2 tablespoons white wine vinegar
- ½ cup (1 stick) unsalted butter, cut into 8 pieces and refrigerated
- 1 tablespoon chopped fennel fronds (optional)
- ½ teaspoon finely grated orange zest
- ½ teaspoon kosher salt

1 Lay the lobster on a tray and put them in the freezer for 15 to 20 minutes (not longer) to sedate them. (This can make handling the lobster a bit easier but if you don't have freezer space for it, you can omit this step.)

2 For the sauce, combine the orange juice, fennel bulb, shallot, and vinegar in a medium heavy saucepan. Bring the juice to a boil over medium-high heat and cook until reduced by about two-thirds, 3 to 5 minutes. Reduce the heat to medium-low and add 2 pieces of the cold butter. Whisk gently and constantly until the butter has creamily melted into the sauce, then add 2 more pieces of the butter and repeat. Continue incorporating the remaining butter in the same →

way, then whisk in the fennel fronds, orange zest, and salt. Scrape the sauce into a small heatproof bowl and set it over a small pan of warm, not boiling, water to keep warm until ready to serve.

3   Put a couple of inches of water in the bottom of a steamer pot or a large pot with collapsible steamer basket. Add the salt, cover the pot, and bring to a boil over high heat. Carefully add the lobster, cover, reduce the heat to medium-high, and steam for 15 minutes, or a couple of minutes more or less based on the size of your lobster (see note). (The meat of the tail should be no longer translucent when the body and tail are separated.)

4   Use tongs to transfer the steamed lobster to a rimmed tray to drain and cool just enough to handle. Serve the lobster as is, or partially portion it first, following steps as noted on page 138.

5   Arrange the lobster on individual plates, pour the sauce into 2 ramekins or other small dishes, and serve alongside for dipping. Have a bowl available for discarded shells.

NOTE: If your lobster are smaller or larger than the 1½ pounds called for here, adjust cooking time as needed, about 2 minutes more or less per ¼ pound difference in weight.

LOBSTER MEAT YIELDS

The yield of meat you'll get from a whole lobster will vary with the season and the size, not to mention the skills and patience of the picker. In rough terms this yield can be in the 20 to 25 percent ballpark. So if you start with a 1½-pound lobster, you may get 5 to 6 ounces of cooked meat from its shells. For lobster tails, my meat-to-shell ratios varied in testing but were broadly in the 50 percent range: a 6-ounce tail should give you about 3 ounces of cooked meat.

Basil, Lobster, and Tomato Sandwiches

Here's a different kind of BLT—but like the original (of which I am an ardent fan), a beacon of simplicity. And it is at its best when the common ingredient, tomatoes, are in prime, peak-of-season form. For other times, I have an all-season alternative (see note). This is an ideal time to go nostalgic and choose old-school sandwich bread. Serve with some extra-fancy potato chips.

Makes 4 servings

- 12 ounces cooked lobster meat (see page 153)
- ¼ cup mayonnaise
- 8 slices sandwich bread, lightly toasted
- About 1 pound vine-ripened tomatoes, cored and sliced
- Flaky sea salt or kosher salt and freshly ground black pepper
- 8 to 12 large fresh basil leaves

1   For lobster tail meat, remove the vein if needed and cut the meat lengthwise into slices about ¼ inch thick. Claw meat can be used as is or halved horizontally if large. Other meat that is in bite-size pieces can be used as is. Discard any bits of shell or cartilage you come across.

2   Spread the mayonnaise on 4 of the bread slices and top with the tomato slices, seasoning to taste with salt and pepper. Lay the basil leaves evenly over the tomatoes and arrange the lobster evenly over the basil. Top the sandwiches with the remaining slices of bread and serve right away.

NOTE: When fresh tomatoes aren't at their most flavorful, you can use the sun-dried variety and mix the components rather than layer them. Coarsely chop the lobster meat and stir it together with ⅓ cup mayonnaise, 2 tablespoons finely chopped fresh basil, and 2 tablespoons finely chopped sun-dried tomatoes (oil-packed or rehydrated dry) with salt and pepper to taste. Add a bit more mayonnaise if it's a little dry. Spread onto 4 slices of the bread, add butter lettuce or romaine, top with the remaining bread, and serve.

Bloody Mary Lobster Cocktail

This recipe is assembled much like a classic shellfish cocktail, though the sauce is a bit different. In addition to having a couple of extra ingredients often identified with Bloody Marys, this lobster cocktail has a much lighter consistency, using tomato juice instead of thicker and sweeter ketchup or chili sauce. All the better to let the lobster be the star. In place of endive, you could use about a cup of shredded romaine or other lettuce to serve as the base for the cocktails.

Makes 4 servings

- ¼ cup tomato juice
- 2 tablespoons minced celery
- 1 tablespoon freshly squeezed lemon juice
- 1 teaspoon horseradish, freshly grated or prepared
- ¼ teaspoon Worcestershire sauce
- ⅛ teaspoon celery seed

- Kosher salt
- 8 ounces cooked lobster meat (see page 153)
- 1 large or 2 small heads Belgian endive, cored and thinly sliced (about 1 cup lightly packed)
- Lemon wedges, for serving

1 Stir together the tomato juice, celery, lemon juice, horseradish, Worcestershire sauce, and celery seed in a medium bowl. Taste for seasoning, adding salt to taste if needed (the tomato juice may provide enough salt).

2 Remove the vein from the lobster tail meat if needed. Cut the tail across into thin slices, and cut other lobster meat into about ½-inch dice; discard any bits of shell or cartilage you come across.

3 Put the endive in small individual serving dishes, spreading it out evenly. Arrange the lobster over the endive, spooning the Bloody Mary mixture over. Tuck a lemon wedge along one edge of each cocktail and serve right away.

Lobster and Artichoke Stew

This light and quick-cooking stew calls to mind the classic oyster stew, like the kind my mom made when I was a kid—oysters, milk, butter—which my dad loved and I wouldn't get near. Shellfish stock adds distinct character, but a good fish stock works well too. As a light meal for two, serve with sliced baguette and romaine salad alongside. In smaller cups, this can be served as a first course.

Makes 2 to 4 servings

- 8 ounces cooked lobster meat (see page 153)
- 1 cup thawed frozen or top-quality canned quartered artichoke hearts (see note)
- 2 tablespoons unsalted butter, plus more for serving
- ½ cup thinly sliced leek (see page 48)
- 2 cups Shellfish Stock (page 183) or fish stock
- 1 cup half-and-half
- ½ teaspoon minced fresh tarragon or thyme
- ¼ teaspoon kosher salt
- Freshly ground black pepper

1   Remove the vein from the lobster tail meat if needed. Cut the tail across into thin slices, and claw meat into 3 or 4 pieces; knuckle meat can be used as is. Discard any bits of shell or cartilage you come across.

2   If the artichoke pieces are much wider than 1 inch, cut them in half, through the bottom core so the pieces mostly hold together.

3   Melt the butter in a medium saucepan over medium heat. Add the leek and cook, stirring occasionally, until tender, 3 to 5 minutes. The leek should not brown; reduce the heat if needed. Stir in the stock and half-and-half and cook for about 5 minutes, bringing the liquid to a low simmer. Reduce the heat to medium-low and add the lobster, artichoke pieces, tarragon, salt, and a couple

of grindings of pepper. Cook to warm everything through and meld the flavors, about 5 minutes.

4   Ladle the stew into shallow bowls, top each with a dab of butter (about a teaspoon, or to your taste), and serve right away.

NOTE: If using frozen artichoke hearts, lay them on double-layer paper towels to thaw and drain, patting them well with paper towels before using. For canned artichoke hearts, you'll need about half of a 14-ounce can. Rinse them under cold water and drain well on paper towels.

Lobster Gribiche Salad

Gribiche is an old-school French sauce that I use here as inspiration for a salad component. The piquant flavors of vinegar, pickles, and capers with hard-cooked egg complement the lobster beautifully. It's ideal for a lunch with salad greens alongside, or as a starter for a dinner party. I find my box grater makes easy work of prepping the hard-cooked eggs and pickles, but you can finely chop them instead.

Makes 4 servings

- 8 ounces cooked lobster meat (see sidebar)
- 3 tablespoons white wine vinegar
- 2 teaspoons Dijon mustard
- ¼ teaspoon kosher salt
- Freshly ground black pepper
- ¼ cup extra-virgin olive oil or mild olive oil

- 3 large eggs, hard-cooked and cooled (see page 181)
- ¼ cup coarsely grated or chopped pickles (about 12 cornichons or 2 medium dill pickles)
- 3 tablespoons finely chopped fresh chives
- 2 tablespoons coarsely chopped capers

1 Remove the vein from the lobster tail meat if needed. Cut the tail across into thin slices, and cut other lobster meat into about ½-inch dice; discard any bits of shell or cartilage you come across. Put the lobster in a small bowl.

2 Combine the vinegar, mustard, salt, and a few grindings of black pepper in a medium bowl and blend with a fork. Blend in the oil until smooth. Spoon 2 tablespoons of the dressing over the lobster pieces and toss gently to evenly coat.

3 Peel the hard-cooked eggs and coarsely grate or chop them. Add the egg, pickles, chives, and capers to the remaining dressing and toss lightly with the fork to evenly blend. Taste for seasoning, adding more salt or pepper to taste. (The lobster-and-egg mixture can be prepared a couple of hours in advance, covered, and refrigerated.)

4 To serve, spoon the gribiche salad onto individual plates, spreading it out evenly, and arrange the lobster on top. Serve right away.

COOKED LOBSTER MEAT

When a recipe calls for cooked lobster meat, you have a few options:

Purchase it as cooked meat, if you can find it (either at the seafood market or online).

Buy raw lobster tails and cook them yourself, planning on roughly 50 percent yield of cooked meat from the raw tails (e.g., 1 pound of tails produce about 8 ounces of cooked meat). Steam 4-ounce tails for about 8 minutes; add a minute or so more for each extra ounce. (Insert a skewer through the center of the meat before cooking if you'd like the tails to be straight, rather than curled, when removed.) Or bake at 350 degrees F for 12 to 15 minutes. With either technique, the meat should be opaque through the center of the thickest part.

Steam a whole live lobster as described on page 143 and pick the meat as noted on page 138. The yield of meat varies quite a lot, for a range of reasons, but can be in the 20 to 25 percent range. So for 8 ounces of meat, you'd want to start with two 1¼-pound lobsters.

Stir-Fried Lobster

with Shiitakes and Celery

Raw lobster meat is best for this stir-fry to avoid overcooked, tough lobster. If you use cooked lobster meat instead (see page 153), add it later in the cooking process to just heat through. For the celery stalks and leaves, those from the interior of the bunch will be more tender and milder in flavor.

Makes 4 servings

- 12 to 16 ounces lobster meat, preferably raw (see sidebar)
- 2 tablespoons mild olive oil
- ½ cup sliced green onion, white and green portions
- 2 tablespoons julienned fresh ginger (from about a 1–inch piece of ginger)
- 2 cloves garlic, thinly sliced
- 4 ounces shiitake mushrooms, stems trimmed, caps sliced (about 2 cups)

- 3 to 4 celery stalks, cut on bias into ½-inch pieces (about 1 cup)
- ¼ cup Shellfish Stock (page 183), clam juice (see page 22), or water
- 1 tablespoon regular or low-sodium soy sauce
- Steamed rice, for serving
- ¼ cup coarsely chopped tender celery leaves

1 Remove the vein from the lobster tail meat if needed. Cut lobster tail meat across into about ¾-inch pieces. Claw and knuckle meat can be used as is. Discard any bits of shell or cartilage you come across.

2 Heat a wok or large skillet over medium-high heat. Add the oil and heat for a few seconds, then add the green onion, ginger, and garlic and cook, stirring, until aromatic, 30 to 60 seconds. If using raw lobster meat, add it and cook, stirring, until the meat is mostly opaque on the surface, 1 to 2 minutes. Add the shiitakes and sliced celery stalks and cook, stirring frequently, until nearly tender, 2 to 3 minutes. Add the stock and soy sauce (and cooked lobster meat, if using) and reduce the heat to medium, stirring until the liquid reduces to a

light sauce that evenly coats the lobster, 2 to 3 minutes. The lobster should be opaque through the center (for raw) or heated through (for precooked). If needed, cook another 1 to 2 minutes.

3   Spoon the lobster and vegetables over steamed rice, scatter with the celery leaves, and serve right away.

REMOVING RAW MEAT FROM LOBSTER TAILS

Some specialty markets may have raw lobster meat available, possibly in frozen form. Plan ahead to thaw slowly in the refrigerator if using this.

Otherwise, you can pull the meat from raw lobster tails. Use kitchen shears to cut through the membrane on the underside. Carefully bend back the sides of the tail, exposing the meat but careful to avoid the sharp points on the shell. Slide a finger between the meat and the shell to begin working the meat away down the length of the tail. After the tail meat has been removed, make a shallow slit along the top of the meat and remove the vein, which is often dark in color. Lightly rinse the meat and dry well.

Yield will vary depending on the size of tail you start with. I get about 60 percent yield of raw meat from the tails I use: about 1¼ to 1⅔ pounds of lobster tails will produce the 12 to 16 ounces meat called for here.

Crab

My West Coast roots definitely show through in this chapter. Dungeness is my hometown crab and the one I know the best of the bunch. Though I was fortunate enough to enjoy fresh-from-the-water king crab in Alaska years ago, and have had some great blue crab experiences on travels to the mid-Atlantic. One notable example was a side-by-side crab-off with freshly caught blue crab and a couple of big Dungeness crab overnighted from Seattle, which I ate with some fellow crab fans sitting steps away from a cove on Virginia's Eastern Shore. The delicious indulgence didn't dissuade me from being a Dungeness devotee. But it did exemplify that—hometown preferences aside—there is very good reason to make the most of any time a good crab opportunity knocks, whatever species it may be.

Dungeness crab reigns on the West Coast, found from Southern California to the Gulf of Alaska. The East and Gulf Coasts are home to the blue crab. Both of these crab evoke strong devotion from their biggest fans, people for whom no cookbook is needed—they know just how they like to cook and eat the beautiful crustaceans. For those not blessed to live within close proximity, we have great seafood markets and direct-order options for sourcing them in whole form, whether live or precooked.

It's fun to see the occasional whole king crab in a live tank, more often in a specialty restaurant than in a retail store. If you see them in a restaurant, consider indulging. It's a memorable experience to be served the whole king crab to share with friends; it may come in a couple of courses prepared different ways.

Prime commercial Dungeness season is winter into spring, though there are pockets of other harvest times—particularly in Alaska summer and fall—through most of the year. Blue crab harvest seasons vary with the region; generally volumes are at the highest over the summer and into fall.

A couple of other crab species you may come across include peekytoe and Jonah from the East Coast, primarily as picked meat. Blue crab are most often available in hard-shell form, but seasonally (or frozen) as soft-shell crab when their new shell is still papery and thin enough be edible. They require particular cooking techniques and are not interchangeable with other crab recipes here. Big, meaty stone crab claws from Florida are harvested mid-October to mid-May.

Because these are wild shellfish, specific seasons and harvest amounts can vary year to year due to a number of factors. Frozen product helps assure it's possible to enjoy most of these crab year-round.

Shopping and Storing

Whole uncooked crab must be alive up to the time that you cook them; the livelier the better when you pick them out at the store. Crab turn orange when cooked, so the color is a quick clue to you when shopping. Live Dungeness will have a bricky-maroon color, and blue crab, a greenish-gray carapace and vivid blue coloring on the legs.

Dungeness in the shell are most broadly available in cooked form, whether whole or in clusters. These will often be frozen crab, though sometimes freshly cooked. If you've bought crab in frozen form, plan ahead to thaw it slowly in the refrigerator overnight. Shells of cooked crab shouldn't have punctures or cracks. Blue crab can also be purchased precooked, with just a quick reheat needed to be ready for enjoying.

King and snow crab are rarely seen whole in stores, particularly live—imagine how big a pot you'd need for that! Instead, they're most often available precooked and frozen, in clusters or leg portions, and for snow crab, sometimes just its claws for an ideal snack serving.

Crabmeat already picked from the shells is a convenient option, ready to use in countless ways. It will be sold in bulk, by the pound, or packaged in tubs. In the case of blue crab, the meat comes in a range of grades—such as jumbo lump, lump, and claw—good for different uses and budgets. With Dungeness, the bulk meat is usually a mix of flakier body meat and nuggets of leg meat. On occasion you may see Dungeness "fry legs" available, just the decadent whole pieces of leg meat perfect for a cocktail or salad.

Cleaning

Crab in the shell should require little cleaning before cooking, perhaps just a quick rinse under cold running water.

Cooking

Cooking crab from their whole, live form is not the most convenient option for most home cooks, if for no other reason than access to them in that form can be limited. For that reason, I have included just one recipe that's intended for whole Dungeness. That and other in-shell recipes also work great with precooked crab, which I expect most readers will use. Precooked crab just needs reheating, so those cooking times will be brief. Taking a few minutes to lightly crack the shells in advance allows extra flavor to penetrate while it cooks.

The remaining recipes call for crabmeat. In a couple of cases I suggest purchasing a specific grade if you have a choice at the store. In most recipes I'll recommend the meat be squeezed to remove excess moisture before using.

PORTIONING COOKED CRAB

Preparing whole cooked Dungeness for serving is pretty easy and doesn't take long once you get the hang of it. It can be messy, though. I do the work in my sink, working inside a disposable bag to collect the discarded parts for easy disposal. Preparing hard-shell blue crab follows generally the same steps, short of the last couple of portioning steps.

1. Use your thumb to lift up the back side of the carapace (top shell) and remove it.

2. Turn the crab upside down and pull back and remove the "apron," a flap of shell lying on the abdomen.

3. Turn the crab upright again; pinch away and discard the feathery gills along either side of the body.

4. Break away and discard the mandibles, or mouth parts, that protrude a bit from the front of the shell.

5. Scoop out and discard the viscera from the body. (The yellowish crab "butter" has devotees, but it's safest not to eat it.) Rinse the crab well under cold water.

6. The crab can be served as is, or halved through the center with a knife. To portion further, cut through the body meat, between the legs, with the claw and first leg in one portion and the remaining three legs in the other.

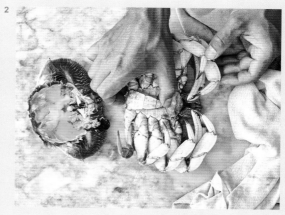

Lemongrass-Ginger Steamed Crab

Adding aromatics such as the lemongrass and ginger here imparts subtle flavor to crab, a quick and easy addition to the basic steaming technique. With the bonus of making your kitchen smell fabulous. For just a couple of live crab, a large pot with a steamer basket in the bottom should work fine, but check before getting to the point of cooking in case it's not big enough and you might need to cook them one at a time. Portioned cooked crab shouldn't be a space issue. Consider serving with steamed or fried rice with sautéed broccoli to round out this meal.

Makes 2 to 4 servings

- 2 Dungeness crab (about 2 pounds each), live or precooked (see sidebar)
- 3-inch piece fresh ginger, peeled (about 2 ounces)
- ½ cup (1 stick) unsalted butter
- 1 tablespoon dry sake (optional)
- Pinch kosher salt
- 2 stalks lemongrass, trimmed, cut into roughly 2-inch pieces and lightly smashed

1   If using live Dungeness crab, you can lay them on a tray and put them in the freezer for 15 to 20 minutes (not longer) to sedate them. (This can make handling the crab a bit easier but if you don't have freezer space for it, you can omit this step.)

2   Finely grate enough of the ginger, preferably on a Microplane, to measure ½ teaspoon and cut the remaining ginger into thin slices. Melt the butter in a small saucepan over medium heat. Take the pan from the heat and stir in the grated ginger, sake, and salt.

3   Put the lemongrass and ginger slices in the bottom of a large pot and add about 2 inches of water. Add a collapsible steamer rack, cover the pot, and bring the liquid to a boil over high heat. Use tongs to carefully add the crab, cover, and reduce the heat to medium-high. Steam the live Dungeness for →

18 minutes, a couple of minutes more or less based on the weight of your crab. If using precooked crab, steam for about 8 minutes to heat through.

4   Use tongs to transfer the steamed whole crab to a rimmed tray and let sit until cool enough to handle, then portion the crab (see page 160). If you steamed crab portions, they can be served directly.

5   Arrange the crab on a platter or individual plates. Rewarm the melted butter, stir, and pour it into individual dishes for serving alongside. Have a bowl available for discarded shells.

COOKED DUNGENESS IN THE SHELL

If using Dungeness in the shell that are already cooked—which you may find whole or in clusters, possibly frozen—you're just reheating and infusing a dose of flavor while doing so. If the cooked crab is whole, I recommend portioning first (see page 160), which makes it easier to fit into the pot and exposes more of the crab to the aromatic steam. Taking a few minutes to lightly crack the leg and claw shells allows even more flavor to penetrate the meat but avoid cracking so much as to break apart into pieces. You can also use king or snow legs (about 2½ pounds or so), cutting them into smaller pieces as needed to fit into the pot.

Crab and Leek Cakes
with Spiced Yogurt

Coriander seed is one of my favorite spices; its slight citrusy character goes well with so many foods. Cilantro is the fresh herbal version of coriander seed, an ideal pairing in the yogurt topping. This is a good use for flake or body meat, but any larger lump meat in the mix makes the cakes even more exquisite. Serve as an appetizer or as a main course with lentils and/or roasted vegetables alongside.

Makes 3 to 6 servings

For the spiced yogurt
- 1 cup Greek yogurt or strained plain yogurt (see note)
- ¼ cup chopped fresh cilantro
- ½ teaspoon ground coriander
- ¼ teaspoon kosher salt
- ⅛ teaspoon Aleppo pepper or red pepper flakes

- 12 ounces crabmeat
- 4 tablespoons mild olive oil, divided, plus more if needed

- 2 pounds leeks, trimmed and cleaned (see page 48), white and light-green portions thinly sliced (about 4 cups)
- 1½ teaspoons ground coriander
- ¾ teaspoon kosher salt
- Freshly ground black pepper
- 1 large egg, lightly beaten
- ⅓ cup plus ½ cup plain dried bread crumbs, divided, plus more if needed

1   To make the spiced yogurt, combine the yogurt, cilantro, coriander, salt, and pepper in a small bowl. Stir well to mix. Taste the yogurt for seasoning and add a bit more salt or pepper to taste, keeping in mind the flavor will develop a bit as it sits. Cover and refrigerate until needed. (The spiced yogurt can be made a day ahead.)

2   Pick over the crabmeat to remove any bits of shell or cartilage and squeeze the meat gently to remove excess liquid. →

3   Heat 2 tablespoons of the oil in a large skillet over medium heat. Add the leeks and cook until very tender, about 15 minutes, stirring frequently. The leeks should not brown; reduce the heat to medium-low if needed. If the skillet becomes dry before the leeks are tender, you can add 1 to 2 tablespoons water, but there should be no residual moisture in the skillet when finished. Stir in the coriander and salt with a few grindings of black pepper. Transfer the leeks to a large bowl and let cool, stirring occasionally to help them cool more quickly. Clean out the skillet for cooking the cakes.

4   Add the crabmeat, egg, and ⅓ cup of the bread crumbs to the cooled leeks and stir gently but thoroughly to evenly blend. The mixture should hold its shape when formed into a cake; if necessary, add more bread crumbs, a tablespoon or so at a time. Form the leek and crab mixture into 6 cakes about 3½ inches in size. Put the remaining ½ cup bread crumbs on a small plate and press both sides of each cake into the crumbs, patting to remove excess. (The cakes can be made up to 2 hours ahead, covered, and refrigerated.)

5   Heat the remaining 2 tablespoons oil in the large skillet over medium heat. (If the skillet isn't large enough to cook the cakes all at once without crowding, cook them in 2 batches, adding more oil to the skillet as needed.) Cook the cakes until nicely browned on one side, 3 to 4 minutes. If the cakes are browning too quickly, reduce the heat a bit. Turn the cakes and continue cooking until no longer eggy at the center and nicely browned, about 3 to 4 minutes longer.

6   Arrange the cakes on individual plates, spoon some of the spiced yogurt alongside, and serve right away, passing extra yogurt separately.

NOTE: If you have regular plain yogurt on hand, you can strain it to use here. It may not be as thick as Greek yogurt but works well for this use. Plan on starting with about 1⅓ cups of whole or low-fat yogurt to get the 1 cup strained. Put it in a fine-mesh sieve, set it over a bowl, and refrigerate for 2 to 3 hours.

Soy-Garlic Grilled Crab

Just a few pantry ingredients create a delicious coating for crab before it hits the grill, making for some delicious finger-licking while you eat too. You can roast the crab instead, in a large oblong baking dish at 475 degrees F until aromatic and heated through, 7 to 10 minutes. Serve with sautéed mushrooms and green beans to make this a meal.

Makes 2 to 4 servings

- 2 Dungeness crab (about 2 pounds each), precooked and portioned (see page 160)
- 2 tablespoons regular or low-sodium soy sauce
- 2 tablespoons mild olive oil
- 2 tablespoons rice vinegar
- 2 cloves garlic, pressed or grated

1 Lightly crack the leg portions of the crab to allow some of the seasonings to work in, but avoid cracking so much as to break apart into pieces. Put the crab in a large bowl or other large container (you need enough room to toss the crab with seasonings).

2 Stir together the soy sauce, oil, vinegar, and garlic in a small bowl. Pour this over the crab pieces and toss to coat as evenly as you're able. Refrigerate while the grill heats.

3 Preheat an outdoor grill for direct medium-high heat.

4 Toss the crab in the soy mixture one last time, then arrange the crab on the grill and cook, turning every couple of minutes, until lightly browned and aromatic, about 6 to 8 minutes. By this time, the crab should be fully warmed, but larger pieces may need a few extra minutes.

5 Arrange the grilled crab on a platter and serve right away.

Crab and Grapefruit Salad

with Crisp Shallots

One medium to large grapefruit should be enough for this salad, but if the grapefruit you find are on the small side, you can use two. If there's not enough grapefruit juice to use in the dressing, just add red or white wine vinegar to make up the difference. You can use other salad greens, or just romaine, in place of this particular combination if you'd like. Feel free to splurge with more crab too. This salad is perfect as a light lunch or first course.

Makes 4 to 6 servings

- 1 medium shallot, cut into ⅛-inch slices
- ¼ cup plus ½ teaspoon extra-virgin olive oil, divided
- 2 teaspoons all-purpose flour
- 1 large grapefruit (about 12 ounces)
- 1 teaspoon minced fresh mint
- ¼ teaspoon kosher salt
- Freshly ground black pepper
- 8 ounces crabmeat
- 4 cups thinly sliced romaine lettuce (about ½ head, or 4 ounces)
- 2 cups watercress leaves (about 2 ounces)
- 1 cup thinly sliced radicchio (about ¼ small head)

1 Preheat the oven to 350 degrees F. Line a rimmed baking sheet with parchment paper or a silicone baking mat.

2 Separate the shallot slices into rings and put them in a medium bowl. Drizzle ½ teaspoon of the oil over and toss well to evenly and very lightly coat the shallot. Sprinkle in the flour and toss well to lightly coat the rings. Scatter the shallot rings evenly on the baking sheet, preferably not touching, and bake until lightly browned and aromatic, 15 to 20 minutes. It's likely that some of the rings will be brown before others; remove them along the way and continue baking the rest. Set the baking sheet on a wire rack to cool, adding back any rings removed earlier.

3   Cut the sections from the grapefruit (see page 79), working over a medium bowl. Use a fork to lift the grapefruit sections from the bowl and set them aside on a plate. Cut or break each section into 2 or 3 pieces. Add any accumulated juice from the plate to the juice in the bowl and measure it; you'll want 3 tablespoons for the dressing. Return that juice to the bowl, add the remaining oil, mint, and salt with a couple of grindings of black pepper. Stir well with the fork to blend.

4   Pick over the crabmeat to remove any bits of shell or cartilage. Squeeze the meat gently to remove excess liquid. Set aside about half of the crab—larger pieces, if there are some—for topping the salad. The rest will be tossed with the greens.

5   Combine the romaine, watercress, and radicchio in a large bowl and use tongs to mix. Add the grapefruit sections, crisped shallots, and half of the crab. Restir the dressing to mix, and drizzle it over the salad, tossing well to evenly mix.

6   Arrange the salad on individual plates, top with the reserved crab, and serve right away.

Fettuccine with Crab and Blistered Cherry Tomatoes

There's no sauce for this pasta, exactly; instead the fettuccine is tossed with cherry tomatoes that have been sautéed until they burst, adding their flavorful juices to the skillet. With crabmeat added and parsley pesto drizzled on top, this is a quick dinner to get on the table for any weeknight—just add a green salad and maybe some garlic bread (see page 132). You can use a classic basil pesto instead of this parsley version if you like, whether homemade or purchased; a half cup will be plenty. Extra pesto can be used in other pasta dishes, added to tuna salad, added to vinaigrette dressing—there are so many uses.

Makes 4 servings

For the parsley pesto
- 1 clove garlic
- 2 cups moderately packed fresh flat-leaf parsley leaves
- ¼ cup finely grated Parmesan cheese
- ½ cup mild olive oil, plus more if needed

- 8 to 12 ounces crabmeat
- 12 ounces dry fettuccine
- 12 ounces cherry or grape tomatoes, halved if large
- Kosher salt and freshly ground black pepper
- 2 tablespoons mild olive oil

1 To make the pesto, pulse the garlic clove in a food processor (a mini processor is ideal) to finely chop, scraping down the sides once or twice. Add the parsley and Parmesan and process until the leaves are more or less evenly chopped. Add the oil about one-third at a time, blending well after each addition, then continue blending until smooth. Transfer the pesto to a small bowl and taste for seasoning, adding a bit of salt if needed (the Parmesan may be salty enough). →

2 Pick over the crabmeat to remove any bits of shell or cartilage. Dry the tomatoes if needed, to limit spattering when cooked.

3 Bring a large pot of generously salted water to a boil. Add the fettuccine and cook until just tender, still with a bit of a bite at the center, 10 to 12 minutes. Carefully scoop out about ½ cup of the water and set aside, then drain the pasta well.

4 Heat the oil in a large skillet over medium-high heat. Carefully add the cherry tomatoes and cook, stirring occasionally, until most of the tomatoes have burst and some skins are lightly browned, 2 to 3 minutes (note that they'll spatter as they cook and the skins burst). Reduce the heat to medium, add the pasta and crab, tossing with tongs to combine, then drizzle in about half of the reserved pasta water to moisten. Cook just until heated through, 1 to 2 minutes. The tomatoes should give off enough liquid to create a light sauce of sorts; add a bit more of the pasta water if needed.

5 Arrange the pasta, crab, and tomatoes on individual plates, drizzle each with a couple of tablespoons of the pesto, and serve right away.

Chilled Crab and Asparagus

with Green Onion Aioli

For such a simple presentation as this, with a couple of star ingredients, it's an ideal time to splurge on lump crabmeat if that's an option. The aioli flavor will be more developed if made an hour or two before serving but is at its best served the same day it's made; see the note for a short-cut alternative to homemade. This makes a wonderful first course or a light supper with a simple fresh pasta dish or grain salad alongside. Note that all parts of the green onions are used, the white and light-green parts in the aioli, the green tops for garnish.

Makes 4 to 6 servings

For the green onion aioli
- 1 egg yolk
- 2 teaspoons freshly squeezed lemon juice
- 1 teaspoon Dijon mustard
- ¾ cup mild olive oil
- ¼ cup finely chopped green onion, white and light-green portions (reserve the dark-green tops for serving)

- 1½ teaspoons minced or pressed garlic
- ½ teaspoon kosher salt

———

- 24 asparagus spears, tough ends trimmed
- 12 ounces crabmeat

1 For the aioli, whisk together the egg yolk, lemon juice, and mustard in a medium bowl. Begin adding the oil a few drops at a time, whisking constantly until the yolk begins to turn pale and thicken slightly, showing that an emulsion has begun to form. Continue adding the rest of the oil in a thin, steady stream, whisking constantly. Whisk in the green onion, garlic, and salt. Refrigerate the aioli, covered, until ready to serve. →

2   Half-fill a sauté pan or large deep skillet with generously salted water and bring the water to a boil over high heat. While the water is heating, prepare a large bowl of ice water. Add the asparagus to the boiling water, reduce the heat to medium, and simmer until evenly bright green and the tip of a paring knife meets little resistance through the end of one of the larger spears, 2 to 3 minutes. Use tongs to transfer the asparagus to the ice water and let sit until fully chilled. Transfer the chilled asparagus to a clean kitchen towel to drain.

3   Trim each asparagus spear to a length of 5 to 6 inches, saving the bottom trim. Return the spears to the kitchen towel, roll them up in the towel, and refrigerate until ready to serve. Thinly slice the trimmed ends and put them in a medium bowl. Thinly slice the reserved dark-green onion tops and set aside to use for garnish.

4   Pick over the crabmeat to remove any bits of shell or cartilage and squeeze the meat gently to remove excess liquid. Add the crab to the bowl with the sliced asparagus and add ¼ cup of the aioli. Toss to evenly mix, without breaking up the crab pieces too much. There should be just enough aioli to hold the crab and asparagus together; add a bit more if needed. Taste for seasoning, adding more salt if needed. Cover the bowl and refrigerate for about 30 minutes to chill and allow flavors to meld.

5   To serve, arrange the chilled asparagus spears alongside each other on individual plates. Spoon a mound of the crab mixture into the center of each raft of asparagus, scattering some of the green onion tops over all. Serve right away, passing extra aioli separately.

NOTE: To make a quick aioli, stir the green onion, garlic, and salt into ½ cup prepared mayonnaise. The flavor will be best if made a few hours ahead, covered, and refrigerated. It won't be quite as richly flavored as homemade, but a decent alternative.

Crab and Endive Gratin

One of my favorite preparations for Belgian endive is the indulgent French classic that wraps it in ham to bake as a gratin with creamy sauce and cheese on top: pure comfort. I find the delicate flavor of crab works well with the endive too. The simple white sauce is typically made with milk. But if you have some shellfish stock on hand, using that here instead of milk adds an extra dose of fabulous shellfish flavor. The gratin can be served in smaller portions as a first course, or as a main course with a spinach salad and sliced baguette alongside.

Makes 2 main-course or 6 appetizer servings

- 8 to 12 ounces crabmeat
- 1 pound Belgian endive (about 4 to 6)
- ¾ teaspoon kosher salt, divided
- Freshly ground black pepper
- 2 tablespoons unsalted butter, plus more for the dish
- 2 tablespoons all-purpose flour
- 1 cup Shellfish Stock (page 183) or whole milk, warmed
- ½ cup grated Gruyère cheese (about 2 ounces)

1   Preheat the oven to 425 degrees F. Butter a 12-inch oval gratin dish or similar shallow baking dish.

2   Pick over the crabmeat to remove any bits of shell or cartilage. Squeeze the meat gently to remove excess liquid.

3   Discard any bruised or damaged outer leaves from the endive and trim the base. Cut each in half lengthwise, through the core. Arrange the endive cut side up in the gratin dish in as even a layer as you can manage; it's okay if they're snug because they'll shrink as they cook. Sprinkle with ½ teaspoon of the salt and a couple of grindings of black pepper. Cover the dish with aluminum foil and bake until the endive is partly tender (the leaves will have darkened in color, the cores still a bit firm), 12 to 15 minutes.

4   While the endive is baking, melt the butter in a small saucepan over medium heat. When melted, add the flour and whisk to evenly blend with the butter. Cook until the mixture bubbles up and has the slightest nutty aroma, about 3 minutes, whisking constantly; the flour shouldn't brown, reduce the heat if needed. Add the warm stock and cook, whisking often, until thickened, about 3 minutes; take care to whisk into the edges of the pan to avoid scorching. Take the pan from the heat and whisk in the remaining ¼ teaspoon salt and a couple grindings of black pepper.

5   When the endive is ready, take the dish from the oven and carefully remove the foil so the steam escapes away from you. Rearrange the endive if needed so it is evenly distributed. Scatter the crab over the endive, then pour the sauce over in a relatively even layer, spreading it out a bit if needed. Sprinkle with the cheese and return the dish, uncovered, to the oven. Bake until the top is lightly browned and the sauce bubbling around the edges, about 15 minutes; you can turn on the broiler for the last couple of minutes to prompt more browning if you like. Let sit for a few minutes before serving.

6   Use a spatula to transfer the endive and crab to individual plates and serve right away.

Deviled Eggs
with Crab and Wasabi

Universally loved deviled eggs take on extra allure with crab added and some peppery zing from wasabi. I prefer the powdered form of wasabi, which stores well in the pantry for making paste as needed for a particular recipe. If you're already a fan of wasabi's peppery punch, start with 2 teaspoons, otherwise use 1½ teaspoons and work up.

Makes 4 to 6 servings

- 4 ounces crabmeat
- 6 large eggs, hard-cooked and cooled (see sidebar)
- ⅓ cup mayonnaise, plus more if needed
- 1½ to 2 teaspoons wasabi paste, plus more if needed
- ¼ teaspoon kosher salt

1. Pick over the crabmeat to remove any bits of shell or cartilage, and squeeze the meat gently to remove excess liquid. Break up large pieces to make stuffing the eggs easier. Reserve a couple of tablespoons of crab for garnish.

2. Peel the cooled eggs and cut each in half lengthwise. Scoop the yolks into a medium bowl and arrange the whites on a serving plate or platter. Mash the yolks with a fork, then add the mayonnaise, wasabi, and salt and continue mashing until smooth. Add all but the reserved crabmeat and stir to incorporate with the yolk, keeping the texture of the crab intact for the most part. Taste for seasoning, adding more wasabi or salt if needed. If the filling is stiff, you can add more mayonnaise as well. If not serving right away, store the filling and egg whites in the refrigerator separately, both covered, for up to 8 hours.

3. Use 2 small spoons to fill the cavity of each egg white with the crab filling, mounding it moderately. Top the eggs with the remaining crabmeat and serve.

HARD-COOKED EGGS

Put the eggs in a medium saucepan and add enough cold water to cover them by about 1 inch. Set the pan on medium-high heat and bring the water just to a boil. When the water boils, take the pan from the heat, cover, and set aside for 15 minutes. While the eggs sit, prepare a medium bowl of ice bath. Use a slotted spoon to transfer the eggs to the ice bath and let cool completely, 15 to 20 minutes.

Shellfish Stock

One benefit of the effort you put into picking crab, lobster, and shrimp from the shell is not only the luscious sweet meat, but the leftover shells that harbor wonderful flavor. For an extra dose of flavor, there's the option of roasting the shells before simmering, which brings out a richer, slightly nutty/toasty character.

Use only shells that have been cooked very simply, without added seasonings. The carapace, or large top shell, from the crab or lobster should be discarded, using shells just from legs and body for the stock. Be sure viscera are removed from the bodies and that the shells are well rinsed. If you only have shrimp shells, you may want to make the simpler shrimp stock instead (see page 184).

You can collect shells from a few different occasions, tucking them into an airtight container in the freezer until you have enough. Or simply make a smaller batch, amending the amount of vegetables accordingly. If you have other vegetable trimmings, such as the tough stalks from a fennel bulb or the dark-green tops from a leek or two, feel free to add them here.

Salt has been omitted from this recipe so you have control over seasoning whatever dish the stock will be used in. This is particularly important if the stock will be reduced, which would amplify its saltiness if it were preseasoned.

For later use, freeze the stock in portions that are easy to grab so you can thaw just what's needed; I usually freeze in quarts. Beyond uses in this book, the stock will be fabulous for recipes such as seafood-oriented risottos, stews, soups, and sauces. →

Makes about 2½ quarts

- About 1½ pounds crab, lobster and/or shrimp shells (not including carapaces), rinsed
- 1 medium yellow onion, coarsely chopped
- 2 large or 3 medium stalks celery, sliced

- 8 to 12 fresh parsley stems (optional)
- 2 or 3 sprigs fresh thyme
- 1 bay leaf, preferably fresh
- 8 to 10 whole black peppercorns
- About 3 quarts cold water

1   As an optional first step, roast the shells. Preheat the oven to 400 degrees F. Scatter the shells in a large baking dish and roast until they are aromatic and lightly browned, 20 to 25 minutes, gently stirring once or twice for even roasting. Transfer the shells to a stockpot. If any juices are baked onto the baking dish, add a cup of warm water and stir to dissolve them, adding the liquid to the pot.

2   If not roasting the shells, put them directly in the stockpot. Add the onion, celery, parsley stems, thyme, bay leaf, and peppercorns to the shells with enough cold water to mostly cover the ingredients, and bring just to a boil over medium-high heat. Reduce the heat to medium and simmer until aromatic, about 1 hour. The water should just bubble lightly rather than roil; reduce the heat if needed. After the simmer, take the pot from the heat and let cool until almost room temperature, which allows more time for the flavors to be drawn from the ingredients.

3   Line a fine-mesh sieve with a thin clean kitchen towel or a double layer of cheesecloth (in a pinch, use a dampened paper towel). Set the sieve over a large bowl and slowly pour the stock through it. Discard the shells and vegetables and set the stock aside to cool. Store the stock in airtight containers for a few days in the refrigerator or up to 6 months in the freezer.

SHRIMP STOCK

As far as stocks go, making a batch of shrimp stock is about as easy as it gets. The thin shells give off their flavor quickly, worth simmering even with just a few handfuls of shells. You can follow the general idea of the shellfish stock recipe, scaling back the proportions (maybe ½ cup each onion and celery, a thyme sprig, a bay leaf, a few peppercorns). Or just simmer the shells in water alone to draw out good shrimp essence worth preserving. Simmer time can be cut to 20 to 30 minutes.

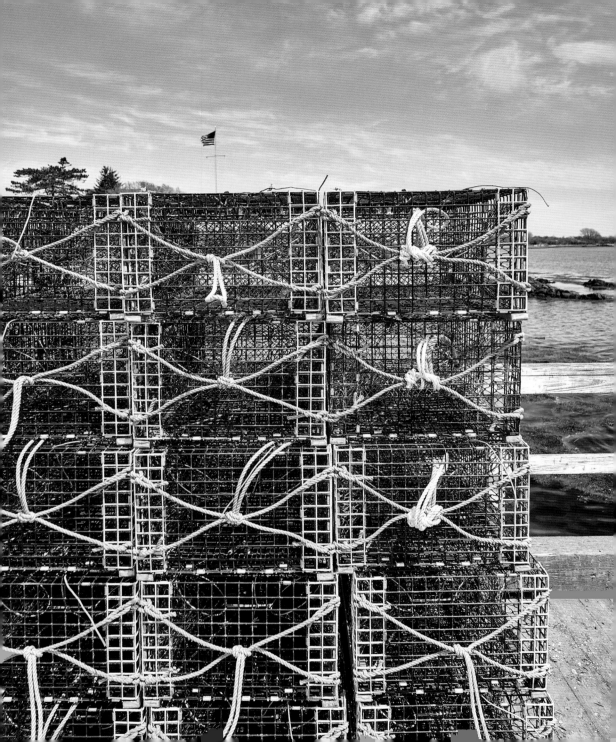

Acknowledgments

First off, I wouldn't have these acknowledgments to write if it weren't for Susan Roxborough, executive editor at Sasquatch Books, suggesting the project to me. Many thanks, Susan, for the nudge. And my great appreciation to the rest of the Sasquatch team who shepherded this book so expertly: Jill Saginario, Tony Ong, and Erin Cusick.

I had a great many interesting conversations with people working in the industry and others who helped me suss out shellfish details shared here. Lyf Gildersleeve from Flying Fish Company in Portland, Oregon; Lissa James Monberg from Hama Hama Oyster Company; Bill Taylor from Taylor Shellfish Farms; and Margaret Pilaro from the Pacific Coast Shellfish Growers Association have been particularly generous with their time for this and other projects. My sincere thanks also to Jim and Mona Stone from Alaska Weathervane Seafoods, Heather Lusk from H. M. Terry Company, Bob Rheault from the East Coast Shellfish Growers Association, Marianne LaCroix from the Maine Lobster Marketing Collaborative, and Laura Diederick from NOAA Fisheries.

To have Jim Henkens's gorgeous images accompanying the book's content is such a joy. Thank you, Jim, for sharing your talents with me once again and bringing out the best in these shellfish.

Cheers to my recipe testers, who provided such valuable insights to help hone the recipes: Cathy Silvey, Dick Wood, Michael Amend, Joanne Koonce-Hamar, and John Starbard. With extra thanks to friend and colleague Susan Volland, who not only helped with testing but was also such a great sounding-board and support through the process. Many other friends piped in with shellfish stories and input. I can't wait to join you for a feast of summertime shedders in Maine soon, Deb!

And while I regularly thank my husband, Bob, for his support, my appreciation in this case is doubled. A couple of months before this book was due, he stepped up to help with final recipe testing while I recovered from a broken leg, me coaching from a nearby stool. I'm incredibly grateful for that extra boost of support this time around. Side note: This non-cook who'd never before minced a shallot created the silky and delicious Orange-Fennel Sauce (page 143) a couple of times flawlessly. So if you think you can't make a butter sauce, trust me: Bob did, and you can too.

Index

Conversions

VOLUME

UNITED STATES	METRIC	IMPERIAL
¼ tsp.	1.25 mL	
½ tsp.	2.5 mL	
1 tsp.	5 mL	
½ Tbsp.	7.5 mL	
1 Tbsp.	15 mL	
⅛ c.	30 mL	1 fl. oz.
¼ c.	60 mL	2 fl. oz.
⅓ c.	80 mL	2.5 fl. oz.
½ c.	120 mL	4 fl. oz.
1 c.	230 mL	8 fl. oz.
2 c. (1 pt.)	460 mL	16 fl. oz.
1 qt.	1 L	32 fl. oz.

LENGTH

UNITED STATES	METRIC
⅛ in.	3 mm
¼ in.	6 mm
½ in.	1.25 cm
1 in.	2.5 cm
1 ft.	30 cm

WEIGHT

AVOIRDUPOIS	METRIC
¼ oz.	7 g
½ oz.	15 g
1 oz.	30 g
2 oz.	60 g
3 oz.	90 g
4 oz.	115 g
5 oz.	150 g
6 oz.	175 g
7 oz.	200 g
8 oz. (½ lb.)	225 g
9 oz.	250 g
10 oz.	300 g
11 oz.	325 g
12 oz.	350 g
13 oz.	375 g
14 oz.	400 g
15 oz.	425 g
16 oz. (1 lb.)	450 g
1½ lb.	750 g
2 lb.	900 g
2¼ lb.	1 kg
3 lb.	1.4 kg
4 lb.	1.8 kg

TEMPERATURE

OVEN MARK	FAHRENHEIT	CELSIUS	GAS
Very cool	250–275	120–135	½–1
Cool	300	150	2
Warm	325	165	3
Moderate	350	175	4
Moderately hot	375	190	5
Fairly hot	400	200	6
Hot	425	220	7
Very hot	450	230	8
Very hot	475	245	9

For ease of use, conversions have been rounded.

Printed in China

SASQUATCH BOOKS with colophon is a registered trademark of Penguin Random House LLC

26 25 24 23 22   9 8 7 6 5 4 3 2 1

Editor: Susan Roxborough
Production editor: Jill Saginario
Photographer and food stylist: Jim Henkens

Library of Congress Cataloging-in-Publication Data
Names: Nims, Cynthia C., author.
Title: Shellfish : 50 seafood recipes for shrimp, crab, mussels, clams, oysters, scallops, and lobster / Cynthia Nims.
Description: Seattle, WA : Sasquatch Books, 2022. | Includes index. |
Identifiers: LCCN 2021015413 | ISBN 9781632174000 | ISBN 9781632174017 (ebook)
Subjects: LCSH: Cooking (Seafood) | LCGFT: Cookbooks.
Classification: LCC TX747 .N56 2022 | DDC 641.6/92—dc23
LC record available at https://lccn.loc.gov/2021015413

ISBN: 978-1-63217-400-0

Sasquatch Books
1904 Third Avenue, Suite 710
Seattle, WA 98101

SasquatchBooks.com

MIX
Paper from
responsible sources
FSC® C001701